Radical
Self-Forgiveness

Radical
Self-Forgiveness

The Direct Path to True Self-Acceptance

COLIN TIPPING

Boulder, Colorado 80306

Sounds True, Inc.
Boulder, CO 80306

© 2011 Colin Tipping

Cover and book design by Rachael Murray

Printed in the U.S.A.

ISBN 978-1-60407-090-3

I dedicate this book to my friend and colleague Karla Garrett, our Director of Education and Training. This is in recognition of her selfless service to the Institute and to me personally. She has also facilitated more Radical Self-Forgiveness workshops than anyone else, and through her compassion and loving presence, she has changed the lives of hundreds of people.

Contents

List of Figures

Acknowledgments

THERE ARE COUNTLESS PEOPLE TO thank for the support I have received over the years in continuing to develop Radical Forgiveness as a healing modality. It was their continuing belief in the efficacy of the process that gave me the resolve and inspiration to extend it to Radical Self-Forgiveness and to write this book. Special thanks are due to my staff here at the Institute, especially Karla Garrett, our Director of Education and Training, whose dedication to Radical Forgiveness and the Institute has been unfailing and total. I also wish to thank Hina Fruh and her husband, Thomas Kiehl-Fruh, for having the faith and courage to make it their own life's work to promote Radical Forgiveness and Radical Self-Forgiveness throughout Germany, Austria, and Switzerland. I am extremely grateful for their dedication to the work and their willingness to create an academy through which to train and certify Radical

Forgiveness coaches and workshop leaders, offering a training of the highest possible standard. I also wish to thank Ireneusz (Erek) Rudniki for doing the same thing in Poland, my dear friend and Radical Forgiveness coach, Irena Rutenberg, having initially introduced the work there, in the country of her birth. I have infinite gratitude and affection for Jaime Schwalb, my editor at Sounds True, who has pushed me to make this a better book than it might have been without her wise counsel and loving support. Similarly, I have to thank Randy Roark, the Sounds True producer of the audio set that complements this book, for whom I have the greatest respect. Finally, no one deserves my love and appreciation more than my wife, JoAnn, whose love and support enable me to continue doing this work.

Introduction

BEARING IN MIND ALL THAT we have achieved in evolutionary terms since the time we walked the earth as an apelike species, you would think we would be feeling pretty good about ourselves in the twenty-first century. Apparently, this is not the case. When the human psyche is examined in depth, it appears that deep down we are all afflicted with a profound and enduring sense of self-loathing.

The twentieth-century Swiss psychiatrist Carl Jung, and many others who have since followed his lead, has shown that both individually and collectively we have repressed a huge amount of guilt and shame about ourselves. Jung referred to this as our shadow. Each one of us has an individualized shadow, of course, but in addition we all share a collective shadow, deeply buried in the collective unconscious. And we absolutely do not wish to face it or recognize it. We are in complete denial about it, and we hate it in ourselves. It is the very root of our self-loathing.

However, just because it is buried deep down in our unconscious mind does not mean that this shadow material is inert or inactive. Far from it, in fact. The truth is that it's constantly trying to come to the surface to be healed, but our fear of facing it is so strong that we often resort to forms of projection and other defense mechanisms. When we unconsciously project it onto other people, we make them wrong for whatever it is we hate in ourselves. This is so common that even political groups, religious organizations, and countries do the same thing. They find enemies on whom to project their shadow material by waging war on them or attacking them in some way.

When we examine conflicts that have occurred in the past and even those that are happening today around the world, it becomes clear in many cases that the very accusations one country expresses against another turn out to be a pure reflection of the former's own crimes and indiscretions and, thus, shame and guilt from past incidents. In my book *A Radical Incarnation*, I made the case that America saw an opportunity to project its shame and guilt about the ethnic cleansing perpetrated against the

Native Americans, and many other crimes against its own people, onto Saddam Hussein and Slobodan Milosevic. In both cases the ensuing wars were opportunities for America to heal its shadow. However, those opportunities were missed as we now know.

From a more spiritual standpoint, it has been suggested that this extremely deep-rooted self-hatred comes from our belief that we took it upon ourselves to separate from God—the original sin. At the moment of separation, so the story goes, we believed that God was very angry with us and would one day catch up with us and punish us severely. This created enormous guilt, and the only way to deal with that guilt was to repress it, and then, if it started to reappear, project it onto others.

Even if we don't wish to believe this story, and I'm not sure that I do, it still largely holds true that much of the wrongdoing that we recognize in those we see as our enemies is nothing more than projections of our own internalized self-hatred. This is still true no matter its cause. The purpose of this book, therefore, is twofold:

1. To heal this self-hatred within the
   consciousness of the collective (i.e., all

human beings together as one), so that we stop projecting it against others in acts of war and other forms of aggression. In that sense, we could also argue that this book is even about creating world peace, saving the planet, and transforming the consciousness of humanity.

2. To help you, as an individual, feel at peace with yourself. Shame and guilt have been shown to carry a very low vibration, and if carried in your own energy field for a long time, they tend to deplete your life-force to a very low level. This creates low self-esteem, apathy, and depression. Radical Self-Forgiveness, therefore, is largely about raising your vibration and restoring your life force back to a healthy balance.

Insofar as we know, when one person makes a significant change to his or her consciousness, it causes a significant ripple effect throughout the collective and contributes to the mass healing of human consciousness. With these practices, you will, in fact, be helping me achieve my mission, which is "to raise the consciousness of the planet through Radical

Forgiveness and to create a World of Forgiveness within the foreseeable future."

Yes, I know this is a grandiose mission statement, and to be honest, when I put it down on paper back in the early 1990s, I really had no belief that it was possible—especially since I had targeted 2012 as the time it would happen. But consciousness has shifted in the intervening years, and I can now envision it occurring quite soon, so long as we keep progressing by raising our individual vibrations day-by-day. And the most successful and expedient way of achieving that is to use the Radical Forgiveness and Radical Self-Forgiveness technology.

It has been suggested to me many times that surely we need to forgive ourselves before we can forgive others. That being so, why would I have waited almost a dozen years after writing the first book on Radical Forgiveness to write this book on Radical Self-Forgiveness? Shouldn't it have been the other way around?

For quite some time the answer I gave was that when you get right down to it, *all* forgiveness is self-forgiveness. My point was, if we are all *one*, then when I do harm to another, I do harm to myself. Thus, it must also be true that when I forgive another, I simultaneously forgive myself. This is the "there but for the grace of God, go I" idea. In other words, there's a part of me that could be or do whatever anyone else can be or do because, again, if we are all one, we all have the same propensities. We are (potentially) all Hitler. So, no matter what someone has done, if I forgive him or her, I forgive myself.

However, this only works for us if we are doing Radical Forgiveness, because it is the only method that provides a practical and easy-to-use procedure that makes collective forgiveness happen automatically. Collective forgiveness doesn't happen with conventional forgiveness. That's because conventional forgiveness works at the human (mental) level, at which judgment and victim consciousness still hold sway. Radical Forgiveness, on the other hand, works at the spiritual level and involves not our mental intelligence or even our emotional intelligence, but our spiritual intelligence. The distinction between these three will be explained in more detail in the following chapters.

It is also one of the tenets of Radical Forgiveness that we purposely (albeit unconsciously, since it is our soul that does it, not our ego) attract into our lives people who will reflect for us those parts of ourselves that we hate and have denied, repressed, and projected. We shall deal extensively with this dynamic later in the book, but maybe you can think of people in your own life who have "pushed your buttons," and recognize that they were mirroring something in you that you may have denied, repressed, or projected onto them.

From a Radical Forgiveness perspective, this recognition would definitely have been the purpose of that relationship. But even if you had realized this, did you ever imagine that you might have brought them into your life specifically for that purpose, and that it was, in fact, an opportunity to forgive yourself? If we can see this and then drop our judgments about the person (i.e., forgive them), we automatically reverse the projection and forgive ourselves.

From a practical standpoint, forgiving others who represent unattractive aspects of ourselves makes self-forgiveness and self-acceptance a great deal easier, because we have something or somebody "out there" to forgive as a representative of ourselves. As we shall see in the chapters ahead, that's a lot easier than forgiving what's "in here."

Turning back to the need for a Radical Self-Forgiveness book, I saw that people who had achieved a high level of success in forgiving others with Radical Forgiveness still found great difficulty in forgiving themselves and remained stuck at that point. Even when they had done the Radical Forgiveness work and were able to recognize that they had created the situation for healing, they still criticized themselves for needing to create the situation in the first place. In other words, in spite of all the work they had done forgiving their persecutors, they found a way to beat themselves up anyway and make themselves wrong. At that point, it became obvious that a different, albeit related, technology was required.

I also realized the need for a specialized practice when I reflected back to my own experience of having gone through two divorces. In the first case, my wife was the one who was the "betrayer," and I was the "victim." She had an affair with someone on our seventh wedding anniversary, and since it happened long before I had discovered Radical Forgiveness, I literally wallowed in victim consciousness for a number of years. But then, after four years of marriage to my second wife, I learned what it was like to be the one who was the cause of the breakup. I discovered that the guilt I felt as the "perpetrator" in this second divorce was a lot more difficult to deal with and lasted a lot longer than the pain of being a victim in the first.

I didn't cheat on my second wife, but she was a lot younger than me and had no children (and definitely wanted them). I'd had my three children and really didn't want more, but I had totally avoided the issue before we got married. We should have discussed it, but we didn't, and that was the cause of the breakup. I beat myself up for being scared to confront the issue when I should have. And to this day, I still notice how much easier it has been to forgive my first wife for the pain she caused me than it has been to forgive myself for creating pain and anguish in my second wife. (She subsequently remarried and had two girls, and we remain good friends.)

In my workshops, I see many situations that cry out for a separate methodology of self-forgiveness. For example, I notice that victims of abuse nearly always blame themselves. They somehow make it their fault, and that is what keeps them stuck, not a lack of forgiveness for the abuser. So, in order to satisfy this need and to fill the void that appears to exist in all of us, I decided to create a methodology for self-forgiveness and self-acceptance that would provide a way to specifically forgive oneself. At the same time, I knew it had to be based on the same basic principles as Radical Forgiveness.

So, in order to test this theory, I created in 2003 an online program for Self-Forgiveness and Self-Acceptance as well as a weekend workshop, both of which have since proven very successful and transformative for participants. This book is based on everything I learned by conducting those workshops and seeing what exactly it is that people need to heal.

If you find it easier to forgive others than to forgive yourself, or you tend to forgive someone for doing something to you and then blame yourself for allowing it, or even attracting it, you are going to find this book to be of tremendous value. If you've struggled with self-forgiveness for years and have been unwilling to grant yourself even a sliver of the grace that you have lavished on others, you will now come to know that you are every bit as deserving of forgiveness as anyone else and will love yourself enough to give it.

Radical Self-Forgiveness offers a great deal more hope than does conventional forgiveness, as it is based upon Radical Forgiveness principles. Let me now explain those principles and summarize the difference between conventional forgiveness and Radical Forgiveness. I will, of course, be expanding on this as we go through the book.

Both Radical Forgiveness and Radical Self-Forgiveness/Self-Acceptance are contained within the same conceptual framework and under the same set of assumptions that have their roots in many spiritual traditions throughout the world. These are:

- While our bodies and our senses tell us we are separate individuals we are, in fact, all one.
- We are spiritual beings choosing to have a human experience but without awareness.
- We live in two worlds simultaneously:
    (1) the World of Spirit, and
    (2) the World of Humanity.
- Life is not random. It provides for the purposeful execution of our own divine plan, with opportunities to make choices and decisions in every moment.
- We create our reality through the Law of Cause and Effect. Thoughts are causes that show up in our world as physical effects. Reality is an outplaying of our consciousness. Our world offers a mirror of our beliefs.
- We, at the soul level, get precisely what we need in our lives for our spiritual growth. How we judge what we actually get determines whether we experience life as painful or joyful.
- Through relationship we grow and learn. Through relationship we heal and are returned to wholeness and truth.
- Through the Law of Resonance, we attract people who resonate with our issues, so we

can heal them. In that sense, they serve as
our teachers.

If this is new to you, don't worry. It is not quite as
crazy as it seems, and it will become clearer as we
go on. And in any case, the method does not require
you to believe a word of it. That's why we call them
assumptions, not principles. All you have to be is a
little bit open to the possibility that life is like this—
that's all.

What this leads to is the idea that there are no
accidents, and *at the spiritual level,* no one is doing
anything wrong or making any mistakes. We are all
getting what we need for our soul's growth, and each
one of us is in service to the other in this regard. That
means there are no victims and no perpetrators.

Obviously, this is very different from conventional forgiveness, which takes no account of the
possibility that there was a spiritual purpose for
what has happened. It references only human interpretations of right and wrong, good and bad, and
has its feet firmly planted in the world of humanity.
And that's fine, of course. But it also takes victim
consciousness as a given, and even though there is
a desire for forgiveness, the core belief is that something wrong happened.

This is what makes forgiveness so difficult and why so few people ever achieve it—especially self-forgiveness. How can you forgive yourself if the core belief is that you have done something wrong or that you yourself are wrong? We do have to confront this issue in Radical Self-Forgiveness, of course, because we are living in the World of Humanity. There are exercises in this book that guide you through this process, looking at how we need to process our guilt and shame when deserved. But at the same time, when we contemplate the much bigger principle that in spiritual terms nothing wrong ever happened, that's when our energy shifts, and we are more able to come to a place of peace about it. Bear in mind, though, that we are not processing that idea mentally. Using the tools, it all happens at the spiritual level.

Part One explores this more deeply, and it also raises some interesting and challenging thoughts about self-forgiveness in general and Radical Self-Forgiveness in particular that lead us to inquire into the very nature of self.

On the assumption that while knowledge is power, self-knowledge is wisdom, the book provides a number of exercises that help you to discover more about yourself or, more accurately, your many selves. I think you will find it fascinating to explore the whole community of characters inside your mind and to identify those who are likely to show up at particular moments.

It will also answer the great philosophical question that always comes up with self-forgiveness: who's forgiving whom? In finally resolving that riddle, we come to see the fundamental difference between conventional self-forgiveness and Radical Self-Forgiveness, and begin to understand why the latter is virtually instantaneous and easy, while the former remains difficult and almost impossible to achieve, no matter how much time you give it.

A large part of the practice of Radical Self-Forgiveness is looking afresh at what you have done that you feel guilty about and then opening up to a new interpretation based on the spiritual reality that *everything happens for a reason*. After that, Part Two of the book focuses on the practicalities. How to actually do it, using the various tools associated with Radical Self-Forgiveness, and how to apply these tools to a variety of situations.

Whereas, prior to the 1990s, few people were interested in self-forgiveness (or forgiveness of any kind) and considered it applicable only to the most pious or the most angelic of people, there is now general agreement that we should all try to achieve it, if for no other reason than it is good for our health and essential to our spiritual growth. As you read, I trust you will find this information helpful and freeing, and that it will add a dimension of joy to the rest of your life.

Radical
Self-Forgiveness

part one

Understanding the Self

1 The Tao of Self-Forgiveness

WHETHER WE ARE TALKING ABOUT self-forgiveness or the forgiveness of others, the idea that forgiveness is extremely difficult and that only special people can do it applies in both cases. In the one case, we perceive ourselves as the perpetrator of some crime or misdemeanor, which leads to a feeling of guilt, while in the other, we perceive ourselves as having been victimized by someone or something, which leads us to feel angry and resentful.

Even though most of us would say we know what forgiveness means, the definition of forgiveness as applied to others is anything but clear, and any meaningful definition of self-forgiveness is virtually impossible to find. That being the case, we are forced to try to understand self-forgiveness in reference to the forgiveness of others.

Webster's Dictionary says that forgiveness is *letting go* of resentment against someone or giving up the desire to punish. Presumably, by that definition, self-forgiveness is letting go of the guilt and shame and giving up the need to dwell on what happened that made you feel that way. But exactly how do you let go? By what method do you *let bygones be bygones,* that being a common colloquial version of the same idea? No one tells you how. And how on earth do we apply that to ourselves?

Webster's also gives the word *pardon* as a synonym for forgiveness. But how can one pardon a wrong? It is not in our power to pardon. To imagine that we have the power to pardon is to presume that we can play God. And if we pardon ourselves, we have to ask who is pardoning whom? Others say "forgive and forget," but how can we forget something that happened that remains burned into our memory? In any case, we need to forgive and remember, not forget. That way we learn not to repeat the error.

Robert Enright and the Human Development Study Group defined forgiveness as "Not only a *decision* or a *choice* to abandon one's right to resentment *(guilt and shame* [my italics]*)* and negative judgments, but an imperative to replace those with compassion, generosity and (self) love." Well, it's one thing to make a decision at the intellectual level to give up these feelings and replace them with compassion, but it's quite another to actually make that happen. Compassion arises from the heart, not the mind.

Paul T. P. Wong, PhD, says, "Forgiveness also involves a compassionate embrace of our enemies in spite of our natural feelings of bitterness, animosity, and fear. It is a voluntary and deliberate act to overlook their flaws and wrongdoings, cancel all their debts, and start a new chapter. And it is nothing less than a very demanding task." For self-forgiveness, we could translate that paragraph to read: "Self-forgiveness involves a compassionate embrace of ourselves as wrongdoers in spite of our natural feelings of guilt and shame. It is a voluntary and deliberate act to overlook our own flaws and wrong-doings, cancel our need to punish ourselves, and start a new chapter." But again, how do we do this?

Charles Griswold, professor of philosophy at Boston University and the author of a book entitled *Forgiveness*, goes even further. He insists there has to be *reciprocity* between the injured and the injurer. In other words, forgiveness has to be two-way. "For it to be true forgiveness," he says, "the perpetrator must offer an apology which has to be accepted. Without some kind of restitution or amends from the perpetrator it does not count as forgiveness."

I cannot agree. Forgiveness is essentially something we do for ourselves, irrespective of whether the perpetrator shows contrition of any kind. As a matter of fact, I think it is counterproductive to tell someone that you are forgiving them. They may not even be aware that they have upset you. I see it as nothing more than a form of manipulation, which is very likely to create a backlash such as a feeling of resentment in that person.

To make reciprocity a condition of forgiveness gives all the power to the perpetrator and compounds victim consciousness. In effect, it puts one in the position of having to say, "If it wasn't for you, I could forgive!" or, "Because you won't apologize, I can never be free of this pain." And if the person is dead, what then? Is forgiveness then out of the question? Of course not.

The confusion arises when people mix up the meaning of two words: forgiveness and reconciliation. With forgiveness, the only one involved is the forgiver, but with reconciliation, a certain reciprocity is indeed required. The injured and the injurer must have an intention to reconcile, which means that the victim agrees to give up his or her anger and need for revenge, while the perpetrator is relieved of his or her guilt by offering some sort of apology or amends.

Both parties need to recognize that an injury occurred to one or both of them, and they should both have a desire to heal the wound and repair the relationship. The agreement to reconcile might include some sort of restitution or reparations.

When an estranged couple try to come back together in order to save their marriage, the work they do is more likely to be in the form of reconciliation than of forgiveness—even if one party has done something for which forgiveness is necessary in that instance. For the relationship to truly come back to a meaningful partnership, it usually requires the give and take that characterizes reconciliation rather than forgiveness.

However, Griswold may well have a point when it comes to conventional self-forgiveness. While it remains in our power to forgive someone for victimizing us, no matter whether the victimizer apologizes or not, when it comes to forgiving ourselves for doing something bad to someone else, for which we are definitely entitled to feel guilt and shame, the attitude of the injured party remains a crucial factor.

Can we even begin to feel self-forgiveness when the other person is not willing to forgive us? Is not the other person's forgiveness some kind of a prerequisite for our self-forgiveness? Should effort be made toward making some form of restitution and amends first? Should we at least apologize before attempting self-forgiveness? Wouldn't it signify that we were bereft of compassion or empathy and without much sense of social justice if we disregarded the other person's condition and feelings and simply went ahead in forgiving ourselves unilaterally, simply in order to feel better?

It would appear then that conventional self-forgiveness has more in common with the concept of reconciliation than does regular forgiveness. In the final analysis, self-forgiveness can occur without true reconciliation having taken place, but without doubt one can only get close to achieving it having exhausted all effort to balance the energy with the injured party. That makes it a doubly difficult proposition.

The arguments go on and on about the nature of forgiveness, but the one thing upon which nearly everyone agrees is that traditional or conventional forgiveness is extremely difficult, and very few people ever manage to achieve it. Self-forgiveness is even more difficult. As if we need more proof of the difficulty of forgiveness, when people actually do genuinely forgive others for some serious crime against them, they appear on TV shows like *Oprah*.

I saw Oprah once listen open-mouthed and speechless when a woman whose son had been murdered claimed that she had forgiven the murderer and had not only visited him for years on death row, but had at some time entertained him for dinner in her own home. Oprah just couldn't imagine how that could be possible and said as much. Neither could 99.9 percent of her audience, I would imagine. I have a name for this kind of forgiveness—I call it *extraordinary forgiveness*. It also seemed to me that the man she befriended, who clearly was guilty of murder, had been able to express his remorse, forgive himself, and hold his head up because she had forgiven him.

I believe the reason conventional forgiveness takes so long and is so difficult to achieve is that in conventional forgiveness we are trying to balance two quite opposite and contradictory energies—the desire to forgive and the need to condemn. This is due to the fact that, with traditional forgiveness, both feet remain planted in victim consciousness. This is true for both ordinary forgiveness and self-forgiveness.

With traditional forgiveness, we take for granted that the perpetrator did something "bad" to the victim and that the victim has suffered as a consequence. The need to blame the other person and to hold him or her responsible remains very strong, notwithstanding the desire to forgive. With self-forgiveness, the assumption is that we did something wrong for which we deserve condemnation, and yet in spite of our having done the crime, we also desire to bestow forgiveness on ourselves.

As long as one feels victimized by what happened, and for most of us it remains self-evident that we were, then in reality forgiveness will remain all but impossible, especially self-forgiveness. It seems clear to me that those two energies cannot be resolved, and this accounts for why Oprah was so incredulous about how that woman had apparently overcome that difficulty. I was, too. The need to condemn will win out 99.9 percent of the time.

We have already established that self-forgiveness is much more complicated than the forgiveness of others in that at least some reciprocity is called for with self-forgiveness. However, there is another level of difficulty with self-forgiveness that needs to be addressed.

WHO IS FORGIVING WHOM?

The term *forgiveness* implies that there has to be one who forgives as well as the one being forgiven.

It requires a subject *(the forgiver)* and an object *(the forgiven)* for it to make logical sense. When we are forgiving others, that condition is met, so there's no problem, but not so with self-forgiveness. The one who forgives (subject) and the one being forgiven (object) are one and the same. Logically, that constitutes a problem. Subject and object can only exist in relation to each other, so it is logically impossible for them to be the same thing.

Who then, when we talk about forgiving ourselves, is doing the forgiving, and who is being forgiven? And to whom or what are we appealing when we ask ourselves for forgiveness? This is not just an interesting philosophical question. It has much to do with the practicalities of self-forgiveness, for it looks as though, in acting as both the forgiver and the forgiven, we are trying to be prosecutor, judge, jury, witness, and defendant all in the same case! Also, unless we know who is talking to whom inside our heads, it will be difficult to have a reasonable conversation and impossible to find any common ground in the argument. That means we have to come up with a reasonable definition of self.

The moment we begin to attempt a definition of self, what becomes clear is that we are not a singular self at all. We are, in fact, a whole community of selves. And the multitude of selves don't always agree with each other. They may have different agendas, which means that at any moment they will be arguing different and even opposing cases. The internal conflict going on inside our heads is likely to be overwhelming.

We might think of some of them as archetypal subpersonalities, all of whom have their own way of being and acting. Our cast might include the critical parent, the professor, the princess, the clown, the snoop, the boss, the damsel in distress, the white knight, the judge, the snob, and so on. At any appropriate moment, any one of those archetypal selves can arise and become dominant.

For example, when we are feeling emotionally vulnerable, the joker is likely to come out strongly in our defense. Making a joke is a great way to deflect the perceived attack and to avoid feeling emotions. If we like to take care of others, our white knight will swoop in on any situation where a damsel is in distress. The princess is likely to show up in situations that trigger her subconscious memories of being treated as a princess by her father.

But there are other selves that were born of our need to survive our early upbringing. These are called *survival personalities*. This term was coined by

Roberto Assagioli, an Italian psychiatrist who, in the early 1900s, founded the spiritually oriented therapeutic system known as psychosynthesis. (As a modality, psychosynthesis is very much in line with Radical Forgiveness.) Assagioli showed that we have within us not just a singular inner child, as has been popularly represented, but a whole host of subpersonalities.

Most of these subpersonalities were created as a way to manage or survive our primal wounds or to compensate for our perceived deficiencies—the basis of our injured sense of self. Clearly, this has tremendous implications for self-acceptance, as well as self-forgiveness. The types of wounds that can cause us to create survival subpersonalities can range from severe physical and sexual abuse, to simply not being recognized for who we are. People raised in seemingly healthy families can also be deeply wounded simply because love was consistently withheld for some reason or used as a form of discipline. This wounding can be very subtle and imperceptible to people outside the family.

Assagioli showed that in order for people to get beyond these wounds and to expand into the fullness of their potential, they must make an *empathic connection* with each subpersonality. That way, each one can reveal itself, be understood, and then be accepted. This is similar to the inner-child work that was popular during the 1980s, where it was recognized that whenever we are triggered, we regress to the wounded child within and act from that consciousness, rather than from our adult awareness.

While the idea of subpersonality has a ring of pathology about it, which makes it seem applicable only to those who have been wounded, the fact remains that every human being on the planet is run by an internal committee. And as we have already noted, this committee is composed of a large number of characters and archetypes, all with their own agendas. However, there are three on which I particularly want to focus, because it is in how these three typically interact that we find the solution to our conundrum about who is forgiving whom. The three characters in question are the resident judge (or judging self), the critical parent, and the inner lover (or self-loving self). Let me describe them for you.

THE JUDGING AND SELF-LOVING SELVES

You are probably most familiar with the resident judge, because that's the one with the loudest voice and is relentless in its effort to make you wrong and force you to accept a huge weight of guilt, irrespective of whether you're at fault. It never stops. Your critical parent is not quite so insistent, but it will treat you like a small child, always scolding you and withholding love as punishment for what it perceives as your constant wrongdoing. This one specializes in shaming you and is the one who delights in dragging down your self-esteem.

Your inner lover is overshadowed and crowded out by these other two, which is why it is probably a lot less familiar to you. You might even be surprised that you even have an inner lover. This is the part of your human self that lives in your heart and will, for the most part anyway, love you no matter what you do. It remains incredibly tolerant of your shortcomings and forgiving of your mistakes, even when they are big ones. It has a huge amount of compassion for you and empathizes with whatever you are feeling. It understands you completely at the emotional level. It knows and identifies with your fears, your anxieties, your joys, your dreams, your loves, your disappointments, and so on. It also knows how to pull together all the other selves in support of your true emotional character. It is, therefore, the great "mediator self."

So, given the fact that there are these different personalities within you, it could be possible to meet the requirement that we need one who is potentially forgiven (an object), if you can find a forgiver (the subject) from the same source. Is it possible that some characters on the committee might agree to bestow forgiveness upon you? Yes, but can you really imagine the resident judge and the critical parent being anxious to do so? Hell no! And guess who holds sway on that committee of yours? No other characters are going against these two! They have too much power, and they will always drown out the inner lover.

Neither the resident judge nor the critical parent will have any compassion for you, nor even tolerance or understanding. Their only interest is in being self-righteous and making you wrong, so of course they are not going to forgive you. Neither one cares whether the guilt is appropriate or inappropriate, and they will accept no excuses. They will assume your guilt is a given and will beat you to death with it.

So, even though we now have a subject (your resident judge and critical parent acting as one) and object (your inner lover), if your only chance of being forgiven depends on whether these two tyrants respond favorably to the entreaties of your inner lover, you're still in deep trouble. Other than in very exceptional cases, the resident judge and the critical parent will always overrule the inner lover and deny you any measure of forgiveness. This is why we find forgiving ourselves to be so much more difficult than forgiving others and why the latter is seldom ever achieved.

With Radical Self-Forgiveness, on the other hand, we have a very different situation—one that offers a great deal more hope. That's because in asking for forgiveness for ourselves, we are making our appeal not to our human self at all, but to our Higher Self— the I Am Self.

When we appeal to our I Am Self, the problems associated with having all those conflicting selves and being dominated by the resident judge and critical parent are neatly sidestepped. When we understand the nature of the I Am Self, it becomes clear why this is the solution we have been seeking.

THE I AM SELF

The I Am Self is the spiritual self that exists above all others, and yet it is the one of which we are least aware. It is often referred to as the "Observer" because it's the one who observes the "I" who is "me."

Our I Am Self is the part of us that remains connected to the Divine, or the All That Is. In that sense, it doesn't really qualify as an individual self at all, because in the spiritual realm we are all one, connected to everyone and everything else, including the Divine. Even so, we can still say that it exists as part of us, as an individualized self that has chosen to be human for a while. It is also the part of us that knows the truth about who we really are, why we are here, and what our purpose for being here really is. It is my contention that our primary purpose for being on this planet and making this soul journey is to expand our sense of oneness. We are doing this by coming to the earth plane, where we can experience the exact opposite—separation. In the spiritual realm, there is only love. Therefore, put another way, our reason for coming here is to experience everything that is *not love* in order to know love. How we actually set our lives up to experience these lessons is explored later in the book, but it is clear that we need a body and a "me" self that is fully human in order to achieve it.

Our I Am Self knows that in spiritual terms there exists no right or wrong, good or bad, and does not identify with the content of our lives, even though it will serve as a guide from time to time. It simply observes and loves us unconditionally, no matter what. It never judges us. It never withholds forgiveness from us, because it knows that there is nothing to forgive.

Our Higher Self communicates its guidance, wisdom, and love for us through that aspect of our own psyche that I refer to as our Spiritual Intelligence. This is quite distinct from our mental and even our emotional intelligence, though these two can provide the entry points to this higher realm of knowing. We receive our Spiritual Intelligence's guidance in the form of physical feelings, intuitive knowing, dreams, and other subtle messaging.

I imagine now that you can see how fundamentally different Radical Self-Forgiveness becomes compared to conventional self-forgiveness and why it works for everyone—not just for special people. When the appeal for forgiveness is made to the I Am Self, it is not subject to debate. The forgiveness is automatic and immediate because the I Am Self knows that nothing wrong has ever taken place, and everything was, or is, in divine order. Period.

The resident judge and critical parent have no part to play in Radical Self-Forgiveness, though they will try to muscle in if they can. But as long as we use the tools that Radical Self-Forgiveness provides, they will have no power, nor any say in the matter. That's because the tools help us to use our Spiritual Intelligence rather than our human mind faculties, and in so doing, they neutralize the influence of the resident judge and critical parent.

RADICAL SELF-FORGIVENESS

In order to explain Radical Self-Forgiveness, it helps to reference it back to Radical Forgiveness, while making a comparison of both to conventional forgiveness.

First and foremost, as already noted, the big difference between conventional forgiveness and Radical Self-Forgiveness and Radical Forgiveness is that these "Radical" versions make the appeal not to our own human self or ego, but to our higher I Am Self through our Spiritual Intelligence. That's what makes them so quick, easy, and effective.

Unlike conventional forgiveness, the "Radical" versions require no skill or special ability. Anyone can do them, even if he or she is totally skeptical— they still work. One does not even have to believe in the central idea that there are no accidents and that our soul has created the circumstances of our lives for our spiritual growth, and that there really are no mistakes in life. All Radical Forgiveness requires is a willingness to at least be open to that possibility.

Since they work energetically at the level of consciousness consistent with our Higher Self, both Radical Forgiveness and Radical Self-Forgiveness operate outside the parameters of time and space. Consequently, results are immediate, and distance is no factor in terms of the energetic effect it might have on all of the people involved, as well as on the situation causing the initial upset.

Second, there is no inherent conflict between the need to condemn and the desire to forgive because, from a spiritual perspective, nothing wrong has happened, and there is nothing to forgive. Consequently, all types of Radical Forgiveness set one free from victim consciousness. From a spiritual perspective, there are no victims and perpetrators—just teachers and students.

Third, there is a proven step-by-step methodology inherent in Radical Forgiveness that is absent in traditional forgiveness. It provides tools that give everyone the opportunity to go through one or more Radical Self-Forgiveness processes—at any time, anywhere, and for whatever reason. The tools are simple and require no training or special ability. One's intellect is involved peripherally in the process, but actual forgiveness does not happen in that part of the mind. With Radical Self-Forgiveness, the practice is handled by our Spiritual Intelligence, which is the part of us that knows the truth of who we are and is directly connected to Universal Intelligence.

If Universal Intelligence means God to you, then it's another way of saying—as most religions do—that it is not we who forgive, but God. In that sense, you could also say that the Radical Self-Forgiveness tools are a particular form of secular prayer. At the same time, though, they work just as well for atheists and secularists, because there is no one who is without Spiritual Intelligence. Everyone has that faculty of mind to the same degree.

With Radical Forgiveness, the decision to let go, release guilt, shame, or resentment, feel compassion for yourself and others, and all the other things people say you should do is not yours (your ego's) to make. It happens automatically when you use the tools, all of which take you through five stages, whether you are doing the work as a victim (Radical Forgiveness) or a perpetrator (Radical Self-Forgiveness):

1. Telling the story (as perpetrator)
2. Feeling the feelings (guilt and shame)
3. Collapsing the story (appropriate or not?)
4. Reframing the story (seeing the perfection)
5. Integrating the shift (physical action)

The first three stages will be familiar to those doing traditional self-forgiveness, but it is the last two that mark the uniqueness of Radical Self-Forgiveness. They spring from a wholly different worldview and, in fact, make Radical Forgiveness more than mere forgiveness, self or otherwise; to experience it is to see the world quite differently and to open to a whole new way of looking at life.

If knowledge is power, self-knowledge is wisdom. So, having resolved some of the issues with conventional forgiveness and given a brief outline of Radical Forgiveness, we shall now examine the nature and structure of the human self in greater depth, so we can respond to the challenges that come our way with greater understanding and wisdom. This human self of ours is, after all, the self that takes us through this spiritual journey we call life.

2 The Human Self

IN THE PREVIOUS CHAPTER, I made a distinction between the spiritual I Am Self and the human self that is "me," and showed that, even though they are intimately connected, they are two fundamentally different selves. Also, I demonstrated that with traditional self-forgiveness we make our appeal to our human self, while with Radical Self-Forgiveness it is our I Am Self to whom we direct our request, which is never denied. The purpose of this chapter is to expand our understanding of the human self by analyzing how it manifests as a complicated community of selves.

THE SELF THAT IS ME
My human self differentiates me from all other humans and shows up in the world as "me" in all my many disguises—that is, all those archetypes and subpersonalities previously mentioned. It is the

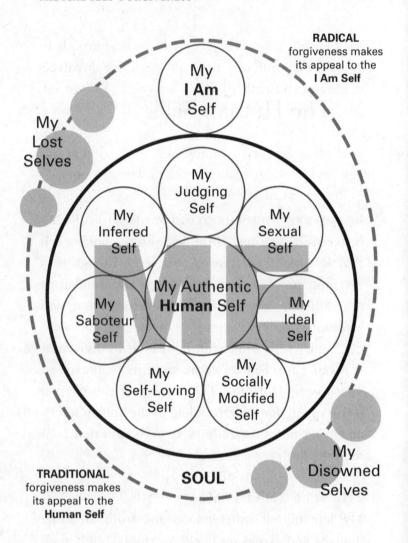

FIGURE 1   Our Multitude of Selves

self that my I Am Self observes and supports. It is the self that feels the pain of separation involved in being a spiritual being in a human body and yet remains willing to go through it for the growth potential it affords.

In many spiritual traditions it is referred to as the ego, and as such it comes presented as the part of us that exists in opposition to the I Am Self and is engaged in mortal combat with it. This leads to the idea, popular in many spiritual traditions, that the purpose of life here is to defeat the ego and, by extension, deny our humanness. This has led to a lot of guilt about who we think we are and makes us feel that being human is a big mistake.

My thoughts run counter to this idea. I see the ego (also known as the "little self") as one of my guides, working in cahoots with the Higher Self. It is the one designated to stay close by our side as we journey through life and to provide the opportunities for growth and learning for which we signed up. Once we have experienced the amount of separation necessary for our journey, the ego will begin to reveal itself for what it is—and what life is really about will become more clear. That's when we begin our awakening to the truth of who we are and truly begin to live from that place— celebrating our humanness and our connectedness with all other life-forms on the planet. This is what it really means to "die to the ego," not to defeat it as so many have suggested.

That said, let us now consider the nature of the human self and how it manifests in a number of different ways, always remembering, of course, that it should not be regarded as pathological in any way. Rather, it should be seen as an expression of our divine purpose for being in a human body. Following I have listed a number of ways in which the self may be formed and expressed—sometimes split and often divided against itself. As you will see, this can make life very interesting and provides many opportunities to experience the separation within. In the exercises that follow these descriptions, you will have the opportunity to identify and observe these different selves within yourself.

The Authentic Human Self

This is the self that expresses your natural essence as a human being. It's who you are at the core of your personality—your basic character—your genetically determined disposition and way of being, both good and bad. Assuming that you don't become seriously altered by traumatic events or in early life experience woundings severe enough to cause a split into subpersonalities, you will be more or less this same person all your life.

The Inferred Human Self

The important distinction here is that, whereas the authentic self is real, the inferred self is a *perceived* self. Even so, it remains a self that can have enormous influence over your life. Your inferred self is a sense of self that becomes generated in your mind, based on the feedback you get from other people. As you observe how people react to you, you say to yourself: "If that's how they see me and treat me, I must be . . ."

While it is true that there are those who go off alone on extraordinary expeditions to discover, from the inside, who they are, most of us come to know ourselves through having others mirror back to us who they think we are. For example, if people tend to avoid us, we might begin to infer that we aren't likeable. If people tend to control us or push us around, we might infer that we are not strong or are not leaders. If people want to be around us and are constantly laughing at our jokes, we will infer that we must be quite amusing and fun to be with. If people tend to flirt with us and come on to us, we might infer that we are charming and attractive.

The real issue here remains one of congruency. If people respond to us in ways that reinforce our own perception of authentic self, then we will feel validated. On the other hand, if people consistently respond to us in ways that are out of alignment with who we think we really are, we will feel unrecognized and misunderstood. That will lead us to feel confused, unsure about ourselves, and resentful.

We see this happen most strikingly with teenagers transitioning from childhood to adulthood, and it can cause an enormous amount of pain and confusion among young people in this stage of life. Since they are in the process of building a self-concept during those years, they are constantly monitoring how others treat them in order to draw inferences about who they are. To add to the confusion, they are likely to be getting conflicting feedback, depending on whom they are relating to at any given time—parents, peers, teachers, authority figures, and so on.

You can only imagine what slaves might have inferred about themselves collectively, as well as individually, having been consistently treated as property, bought and sold, tortured and abused, and generally disregarded by other human beings. History shows that, even after becoming free, peoples who had been enslaved at one point or another passed on feelings of low self-worth for many generations afterward.

We can also get a lot of mixed messages depending on the variety of people and circumstances that we encounter. We might get very positive messages about ourselves in one situation, and then when we mix with a different crowd, we may experience quite the opposite. This can be incredibly confusing for our inferred selves. The point about the inferred self is that it remains in a state of constant flux, unlike the authentic self, which hardly changes at all. For that reason alone, the inferred self has the capacity to cause uncertainty and confusion, and it can feed on those vulnerabilities in a magnitude of ways.

The more uncertain we become about ourselves, the more sensitive we become to others around us, and the more likely we are to try being someone we are not. We become very concerned about what others think about us, and we continually seek approval from everyone around us. As a result, we become susceptible to guilt, both self-imposed and suggested by others, and to heightened levels of shame and humiliation.

In comparing our inferred self with our authentic self, we can gain some tremendous wisdom. If we find that the two are congruent, then we feel validated.

However, should we discover that there is a sufficient disparity between our selves that is causing confusion, we can begin to work on bringing them back together. Much of this reunion will happen automatically as a result of Radical Self-Forgiveness and Radical Self-Acceptance work; however, there is one question you can ask of yourself right now: what am I projecting about myself that is *not* true but that other people are seeing as being the truth about me?

The Ideal Self

This is the self we would really like to be. Whereas our inferred self was a perceived self, the ideal self is a *fantasy* self. Who we model ourselves on is often an indication of our ideal self. Film stars, sports personalities, statesmen, members of the media, and the like are examples of people upon whom we might model ourselves.

Such ideals are usually quite harmless and, in our youth anyway, serve to help us develop our sense of identity. However, once again, it is a question of congruency. If your ideal self is one that helps to develop more of your authentic self or gives you something to aim for that would be in alignment with your authentic self and purpose, then it can be an incredibly powerful force of self-integration.

On the other hand, if the discrepancies between your ideal self and your authentic self are too expansive, or if the qualities of each are completely different, a significant amount of dissonance will occur. That, in turn, will lead to confusion, disappointment, and a profound sense of dissatisfaction with self. In the spirit of self-knowledge being wisdom, it is a good idea to make sure your ideal self and your authentic self are mutually supportive. Take a moment to consider your role models—do you notice any type of congruency or lack thereof?

Assuming that there is congruence, the ideal self offers a great deal of assistance in helping you grow into your full potential. It is the self that is able to hold a vision of you in the future and helps to propel you in that direction. It will set goals and, through the Law of Attraction, help manifest your dreams. It is a powerful self, but it needs to be monitored to make sure its prodigious energy is properly harnessed for your benefit.

The Socially Modified Self
This is the self that is not really us, but that we may have become in order to be accepted—the person others have wanted us to be. This is the socially constructed self we have become in order to fit in

socially or within a family—even though it is not really us.

As members of any group, we agree to give up some aspects of ourselves in order to conform to certain group norms. Anyone who was brought up in a severely dysfunctional family is likely to have developed a highly modified self, which was simply formed as a way to survive. This conformity occurs at all levels of society: at work, school, church, political situations, in the media, and so on. That's because we are all social animals and are willing to adhere to group norms in order to be socially accepted.

But how much of our individual self-expression are we willing to give up in return for the comfort of being part of these groups? Suppose we are drawn to a particular religious group but have to conform to some very strict rules? Suppose we want to be a monk or a priest or a rabbi? Are we willing to modify who we are for certain purposes? The answer depends on a great many factors and might easily be "yes" if that choice is in line with our overall sense of self and purpose. However, we must ensure that the answer is "no" at the point where, in order to conform, we find ourselves failing to remember our own integrity. To be in integrity means to be whole and complete. If we fall out of integrity with ourselves, we are essentially living a lie. When we are out of integrity with ourselves, our authentic self is completely impaired. When we are inauthentic, we begin to sell ourselves short and chip away at our sense of self. Others will see through us and will eventually reject us. It is clear that we cannot live an inauthentic life for very long. The way to restore our integrity is to reclaim our true selves.

Having looked at how your human self is initially formed, modified according to how others perceive you, and then further adjusted in order to conform to social demands, use the following exercises to discover the complexities of who you are and where there is dissonance or incongruency in your own life.

Exercise #1: Identifying Your Authentic Self

Imagine that you had to describe yourself in detail to someone who has never met you or interacted with you in any way. In a journal or notebook, or in the notes section that follows, describe your authentic (real) self in such a way that a person reading it would get a genuine feel for your natural way of being, the truth of who you are at the very core of your being, your fundamental character, and the essence of who you are in this world.

You might check some of the qualities listed below that apply to you, some or most of the time, and then use them as starting points for your written description. You'll probably be surprised at how little you really know yourself.

I Am	*Notes*
☐ Introverted	_____
☐ Extroverted	_____
☐ Talkative	_____
☐ Quiet	_____
☐ Happy-go-lucky	_____
☐ Melancholy	_____
☐ Intellectual	_____
☐ Emotional	_____
☐ Excitable	_____
☐ Controlling	_____
☐ A strong leader	_____
☐ A supporter	_____
☐ Team oriented	_____
☐ Individualistic	_____
☐ Manipulating	_____
☐ Courageous	_____

I AM	*NOTES*
☐ Fearful	_____
☐ Seductive	_____
☐ Shy	_____
☐ Nervous	_____
☐ Narcissistic	_____
☐ Analytical	_____
☐ Generous	_____
☐ Grouchy	_____
☐ Stingy	_____
☐ Combative	_____
☐ Curious	_____
☐ Passionate	_____
☐ Dull	_____
☐ Theatrical	_____
☐ A dreamer	_____
☐ Ambitious	_____
☐ A gambler	_____
☐ Sexy	_____
☐ A nurturer	_____
☐ Forgiving	_____
☐ Blunt	_____

I Am   Notes

☐ Competitive   _____

☐ Indecisive   _____

☐ Noncommittal   _____

☐ Practical   _____

☐ Obedient   _____

☐ Rebellious   _____

☐ Distrustful   _____

☐ Trusting   _____

☐ Caring   _____

☐ Inflexible   _____

☐ Energetic   _____

☐ Optimistic   _____

☐ Pessimistic   _____

☐ Persistent   _____

☐ Graceful   _____

☐ Clumsy   _____

☐ Judgmental   _____

☐ Hardworking   _____

☐ Lazy   _____

☐ _____   _____

☐ _____   _____

Exercise #2: Identifying Your (False) Inferred Self
Go over the same list and check any traits that you did *not* include as part of your authentic self, but that could be considered by others to be true about you (i.e., inferred qualities).

I AM NOT THESE,
THOUGH PEOPLE
THINK I AM　　　　*NOTES*

- ☐ Introverted　＿＿＿＿＿＿＿＿＿＿＿
- ☐ Extroverted　＿＿＿＿＿＿＿＿＿＿＿
- ☐ Talkative　＿＿＿＿＿＿＿＿＿＿＿＿
- ☐ Quiet　＿＿＿＿＿＿＿＿＿＿＿＿＿
- ☐ Happy-go-lucky ＿＿＿＿＿＿＿＿＿
- ☐ Melancholy　＿＿＿＿＿＿＿＿＿＿＿
- ☐ Intellectual　＿＿＿＿＿＿＿＿＿＿＿
- ☐ Emotional　＿＿＿＿＿＿＿＿＿＿＿
- ☐ Excitable　＿＿＿＿＿＿＿＿＿＿＿
- ☐ Controlling　＿＿＿＿＿＿＿＿＿＿＿
- ☐ A strong leader ＿＿＿＿＿＿＿＿＿
- ☐ A supporter　＿＿＿＿＿＿＿＿＿＿＿
- ☐ Team oriented　＿＿＿＿＿＿＿＿＿＿
- ☐ Individualistic　＿＿＿＿＿＿＿＿＿＿
- ☐ Manipulating　＿＿＿＿＿＿＿＿＿＿

I Am Not These, Though People Think I Am	NOTES
☐ Courageous	_____
☐ Fearful	_____
☐ Seductive	_____
☐ Shy	_____
☐ Nervous	_____
☐ Narcissistic	_____
☐ Analytical	_____
☐ Generous	_____
☐ Grouchy	_____
☐ Stingy	_____
☐ Combative	_____
☐ Curious	_____
☐ Passionate	_____
☐ Dull	_____
☐ Theatrical	_____
☐ A dreamer	_____
☐ Ambitious	_____
☐ A gambler	_____
☐ Sexy	_____
☐ A nurturer	_____

I Am Not These,
Though People
Think I Am   NOTES

☐ Forgiving   _____

☐ Blunt   _____

☐ Competitive   _____

☐ Indecisive   _____

☐ Noncommittal   _____

☐ Practical   _____

☐ Obedient   _____

☐ Rebellious   _____

☐ Distrustful   _____

☐ Trusting   _____

☐ Caring   _____

☐ Inflexible   _____

☐ Energetic   _____

☐ Optimistic   _____

☐ Pessimistic   _____

☐ Persistent   _____

☐ Graceful   _____

☐ Clumsy   _____

☐ Judgmental   _____

☐ Hardworking   _____

I Am Not These,
Though People
Think I Am   NOTES

☐ Lazy   _____

☐ _____   _____

☐ _____   _____

Now, write in your journal a statement that describes how you tend to be seen as a certain kind of person, with the qualities you have checked (both good and bad) that are *not* an accurate reflection of who you are. Note how it makes you feel that people treat you as if you were those things. Write a statement acknowledging that you may actually be projecting those qualities for others to perceive, even though they are not true.

This is a very important exercise because, rather than blaming the people "out there," you are taking full responsibility for the potential that you created the disparity. You are recognizing that people react according to what you transmit energetically— whatever you are projecting comes back to you. So, rather than let it feed on itself and become seriously compounded, try to determine what you are projecting and why.

You'll almost certainly discover that you are projecting some kind of negative belief about yourself that you learned at one time. Even though that belief goes against the truth of your authentic self, in one way or another, it has been integrated into part of who you are now. For example, suppose your mother had made a rule that you were not allowed to help yourself to cookies from the cookie jar. Then you noticed that your little brother was crying because he was hungry, so you thought raiding the jar for just one cookie to give to him would justify breaking the rule. Your mother then caught you with your hand in the cookie jar. She became enraged and punished you unmercifully for being untrustworthy and deceitful. She beat into you that you were untrustworthy to such an extent that you came to believe it.

Later in life, you will project that as energy causing those around you to have nagging doubts about your trustworthiness. Although they can never quite understand it, nor do they have any real reason for it, the feeling will remain. You might find yourself being passed over for responsible positions at work or having security clearances denied for no apparent reason. Boyfriends or girlfriends might doubt your fidelity to a relationship and always feel the need to be checking up on you. The Radical Self-Forgiveness and Radical Self-Acceptance processes will take care of removing all these old beliefs that create a false perception of self, in making it more likely that people react to you in a way that aligns more with your true self.

Exercise #3: Identifying Your Ideal Self

Review the following list of only positive qualities. Check the ones that you already have and those you would ideally like to have to construct the ideal you. Assume you are totally free to be who you want to be, without limitation.

I Am	Notes
☐ Introverted	_____
☐ Extroverted	_____
☐ Talkative	_____
☐ Quiet	_____
☐ Happy-go-lucky	_____
☐ Intellectual	_____
☐ Emotional	_____
☐ Excitable	_____
☐ A strong leader	_____
☐ A supporter	_____

I Am	Notes
☐ Team oriented	_____
☐ Courageous	_____
☐ Seductive	_____
☐ Analytical	_____
☐ Generous	_____
☐ Curious	_____
☐ Passionate	_____
☐ Theatrical	_____
☐ A dreamer	_____
☐ Ambitious	_____
☐ A gambler	_____
☐ Sexy	_____
☐ A nurturer	_____
☐ Forgiving	_____
☐ Competitive	_____
☐ Practical	_____
☐ Rebellious	_____
☐ Trusting	_____
☐ Caring	_____
☐ Energetic	_____
☐ Optimistic	_____

I Am	*Notes*
☐ Persistent	_____
☐ Graceful	_____
☐ Hardworking	_____
☐ _____	_____
☐ _____	_____
☐ _____	_____
☐ _____	_____

List some of the people you admire and indicate the main qualities they have that you wish to have. Then, indicate whether each person is a good role model for you.

Person	*Qualities*	*Role Model?*
_____	_____	_____
_____	_____	_____
_____	_____	_____
_____	_____	_____
_____	_____	_____
_____	_____	_____
_____	_____	_____
_____	_____	_____

PERSON	QUALITIES	ROLE MODEL?
_____	_____	_____
_____	_____	_____
_____	_____	_____
_____	_____	_____
_____	_____	_____
_____	_____	_____

Assuming you are not already doing what you consider to be your divine purpose, write in your journal what you would want to be doing with your life now if you were totally free to choose.

Construct a word picture in your journal of your ideal self. Describe your ideal physical self and the kind of mental, emotional, and spiritual qualities that you might have and how these might be expressed in how you live. What kind of disposition would you ideally like to have and what skills and abilities? Push the envelope and exaggerate to some extent, but let it still be you. Mention your role models and the ways in which you would like to be like them.

Begin by saying: "The way I like to imagine myself being is . . . "

Exercise #4: Identifying Your Modified Self

Review the following list and identify the qualities that you have adopted or rejected in order to conform or feel like you really belong, and to be accepted by your family, church, peer group, and so on. Note: the qualities can vary depending on the group, but include them all.

Introverted	☐ Adopted	☐ Rejected
Extroverted	☐ Adopted	☐ Rejected
Talkative	☐ Adopted	☐ Rejected
Quiet	☐ Adopted	☐ Rejected
Happy-go-lucky	☐ Adopted	☐ Rejected
Melancholy	☐ Adopted	☐ Rejected
Intellectual	☐ Adopted	☐ Rejected
Emotional	☐ Adopted	☐ Rejected
Excitable	☐ Adopted	☐ Rejected
Controlling	☐ Adopted	☐ Rejected
A strong leader	☐ Adopted	☐ Rejected
A supporter	☐ Adopted	☐ Rejected
Team oriented	☐ Adopted	☐ Rejected
Individualistic	☐ Adopted	☐ Rejected
Manipulating	☐ Adopted	☐ Rejected

Courageous	☐ Adopted	☐ Rejected
Fearful	☐ Adopted	☐ Rejected
Seductive	☐ Adopted	☐ Rejected
Shy	☐ Adopted	☐ Rejected
Nervous	☐ Adopted	☐ Rejected
Narcissistic	☐ Adopted	☐ Rejected
Analytical	☐ Adopted	☐ Rejected
Generous	☐ Adopted	☐ Rejected
Grouchy	☐ Adopted	☐ Rejected
Stingy	☐ Adopted	☐ Rejected
Combative	☐ Adopted	☐ Rejected
Curious	☐ Adopted	☐ Rejected
Passionate	☐ Adopted	☐ Rejected
Dull	☐ Adopted	☐ Rejected
Theatrical	☐ Adopted	☐ Rejected
A dreamer	☐ Adopted	☐ Rejected
Ambitious	☐ Adopted	☐ Rejected
A gambler	☐ Adopted	☐ Rejected
Sexy	☐ Adopted	☐ Rejected
A nurturer	☐ Adopted	☐ Rejected
Forgiving	☐ Adopted	☐ Rejected
Blunt	☐ Adopted	☐ Rejected

Competitive	☐ Adopted	☐ Rejected
Indecisive	☐ Adopted	☐ Rejected
Noncommittal	☐ Adopted	☐ Rejected
Practical	☐ Adopted	☐ Rejected
Obedient	☐ Adopted	☐ Rejected
Rebellious	☐ Adopted	☐ Rejected
Distrustful	☐ Adopted	☐ Rejected
Trusting	☐ Adopted	☐ Rejected
Caring	☐ Adopted	☐ Rejected
Inflexible	☐ Adopted	☐ Rejected
Energetic	☐ Adopted	☐ Rejected
Optimistic	☐ Adopted	☐ Rejected
Pessimistic	☐ Adopted	☐ Rejected
Persistent	☐ Adopted	☐ Rejected
Graceful	☐ Adopted	☐ Rejected
Clumsy	☐ Adopted	☐ Rejected
Judgmental	☐ Adopted	☐ Rejected
Hardworking	☐ Adopted	☐ Rejected
Lazy	☐ Adopted	☐ Rejected
_____	☐ Adopted	☐ Rejected
_____	☐ Adopted	☐ Rejected
_____	☐ Adopted	☐ Rejected

In the process of creating the socially modified self, we often lose many parts of ourselves. These selves are distinct and deserve to be recognized in their own right—I refer to them as our "lost selves." This is one of the subjects of the next chapter.

3 Other Aspects of Self

THERE ARE PARTS OF OURSELVES that for various reasons have either split off, become divided, or been disowned altogether. It is important from both a self-forgiveness and self-acceptance point of view that we understand how and why this happened, always remembering, of course, that there is divine purpose in everything. There are no accidents and no mistakes.

THE LOST SELVES
Our lost selves are the specific parts of ourselves that we have shut down or traded away, both as children and since becoming adults, in exchange for acceptance, love, power, money, and so on. They are the parts that we might have willingly cast off during the process of creating the socially modified self.

Again, in the interest of self-knowledge, it is worthwhile to take a look at what parts of yourself you might have given or traded away—and for what reasons. The most common scenario is trading our integrity or self-respect for money, power, status, or success; however, this can be applied to a whole host of things that you may have lost or traded away. The following exercise will give you the opportunity to discover your own lost selves, but here are some examples:

> "I gave up my usual friendly, gregarious self in order to appease and stay married to a jealous man."

> "In order to fit in at work, I have had to leave my fun-loving, creative self at the door and do everything according to the book. As a result, I am no longer the fun-loving, creative person I used to be, even when I am not at work."

> "In order to please my family, I gave up my professional career to have kids, even though my career was my passion. I love my children but have no passion for parenthood. I traded away my passion."

> "I used to be a risk-taker and got a real buzz from the excitement, but since I am now

responsible for a wife and family, I have to play it safe all the time."

"My fulfillment is in being a musician, but I have taken a job that gives me steady income and leaves me no time to play my music. I traded my fulfillment and musical creativity for a steady income."

Exercise #5: Identifying Your Lost Selves

Reflect on the parts of your authentic self that you have lost by giving them up or shutting them down or trading them away for love, money, power, status, or something similar, and expand on them in the notes field.

LOST SELVES	NOTES
☐ Sexuality	_____
☐ Humor	_____
☐ Innocence	_____
☐ Integrity	_____
☐ Honesty	_____
☐ Trust	_____
☐ Curiosity	_____
☐ Feelings	_____
☐ Passion	_____

Lost Selves	Notes
☐ Life dream	_____
☐ Ambition	_____
☐ Risk-taking	_____
☐ Generosity	_____
☐ Freedom	_____
☐ Parenthood	_____
☐ Happiness	_____
☐ Peace	_____
☐ Fulfillment	_____
☐ _____	_____
☐ _____	_____
☐ _____	_____
☐ _____	_____
☐ _____	_____

As you begin to examine how you might have given up or traded away certain parts of yourself, it is likely that you'll experience feelings of deep sadness and regret. That's OK. Those feelings need to be felt. You might also feel some guilt, which is OK, too. That said, be mindful of the tendency to compound additional guilt atop what you may already be carrying. This is particularly applicable if you are prone to excess guilt and to beating yourself up all the time. Any guilt about your lost selves will be dispersed later through the Radical Self-Forgiveness process, so there's no point in magnifying what is already there.

Complete the exercise by finishing this sentence: "If I had the chance to do it all over, the one thing I would not trade away again would be . . ."

_____

_____

_____

_____

_____

THE DISOWNED SELVES

Our disowned selves are the parts of ourselves that we have rejected as unacceptable and have put completely out of sight and out of mind. We accomplish this through the mechanism of repression. That means that we have pushed them so deep down in the subconscious mind that we have absolutely no awareness of them whatsoever.

Repression is not the same as suppression. When we suppress parts of ourselves, we know they are still there. This would be true of our lost selves. We know those parts exist in us, but we intentionally keep them suppressed. Conversely, those parts of ourselves that we have disowned and repressed are out of our awareness altogether. Carl Jung referred to this repressed material as our shadow. Let's look at how these parts of ourselves initially got denied, rejected, and then disowned.

When we were growing up and looking for approval and love from those around us, most notably our parents, we soon learned which of our attributes won us love and approval and which did not. Out of a sense of survival, we selected the most *approved* attributes to live from and quickly disowned the others.

From the acceptable list, we created the socially modified self that we present to the world, and we dumped the rest into our shadow. It's likely that we've added even more material to our shadow as we've developed, but most of our disowned selves were repressed early as a result of our being shamed over them. Having shifted all the *unapproved* attributes into our shadow and repressed them, we might think they are safely buried and inactive. They are not. Attached to every one of them is an energy, which is both active and reactive. Each attribute has the ability to rise up from the depths of our unconscious to be recognized and accepted.

For that reason, we remain ever fearful of our shadow, and we do everything we can to avoid coming to terms with it. The act of repressing it is an avoidance strategy. But an even better way to avoid dealing with our shadow material is to project it onto someone else. In other words, we symbolically take it out of ourselves, project it onto someone or something else *out there,* and then convince ourselves that we no longer have it.

Here's how it works: we first find someone who seems to have a lot of the qualities we hate in ourselves. Next, we criticize or judge him or her unmercifully for having those qualities, unaware, of course, that they are our very own attributes. We then become angry and self-righteous and go to great lengths to make the person wrong, and to punish him or her if possible. With our focus strongly set on the "bad" person out there, the need to see what is "in here" is neatly sidestepped and avoided.

Projection is a powerful defense mechanism. It has the potential to keep us stuck in self-loathing, because it automatically prevents us from recognizing and accepting a significant part of ourselves. Nevertheless, it does offer us a way to retrieve our disowned selves. Once we understand the mechanism of projection and can recognize when we are doing it—that is, when we are criticizing another for our own shortcomings—we can decide to reverse the projection.

When we become more aware of our tendencies to project, we are in effect recognizing the principle "If you spot it, you've got it." We reclaim our projection by recognizing the person we are judging as someone who has come into our lives to mirror what we have disowned and to give us the opportunity to see it and welcome it back with love and acceptance.

The following exercise will help you discover some of your disowned selves.

Exercise #6: Identifying Your Disowned Selves

It would make no sense, in this instance, for you to make a list of your disowned selves, since by definition they are unknown to you. Having been repressed, they live not in your conscious mind but in your subconscious mind, almost completely out of your awareness. Not to worry, though. There is a perfectly good and reliable way to discover them by doing a reverse projection exercise. The procedure is as follows.

Think of two people you dislike or disapprove of in many ways and make a list of the qualities they represent that you find most objectionable. They can be people you know personally or personalities you only see in the media. They may be dead or alive. The important thing is that you feel very judgmental and critical of them for a number of reasons. Try to list about ten traits if you can. There's no need to mention the actual name of either person.

PERSON 1   PERSON 2

_____   _____
_____   _____
_____   _____
_____   _____
_____   _____
_____   _____
_____   _____
_____   _____
_____   _____
_____   _____

Claim each one of these traits as disowned parts of yourself that you have denied, repressed, and projected onto these two people.

The point here is to understand that if you were to make a list of your disowned selves, every one of the qualities listed above would top the list. That's because the principle is, as I have already said, "If you spot it, you've got it." You are seeing in these two people what you despise in yourself and have ultimately disowned. In effect, you are looking in the mirror.

However, before you throw this book at the wall in disgust, bear in mind that the mirror can trick you. While with some people the reflection may be obvious, with others it may not be a direct correlation. What you see in the other person may only be symbolic or representative of something within you, and it is difficult to know what exactly that might be.

So don't waste energy trying to figure it out. Just accept that everything that you have listed is indicative, either directly or indirectly, of your disowned selves, and that these qualities are showing up to be loved and accepted just the way they are. Do *not* make yourself guilty again for creating them. That just perpetuates the cycle.

THE SABOTEUR SELF

This is the self that is constantly checking your subconscious mind to make sure that whatever you are doing, thinking, or planning at the conscious level matches all the beliefs, ideas, attitudes, concepts, prejudices, and other content that exists at the subconscious level. If there is not a good match, this self will sabotage you in every way possible. It will sabotage your relationships, your finances, and every other area of your life if what you are doing, thinking, or planning is not in accordance with every belief that already exists in your subconscious.

For instance, if, as a consequence of having witnessed your parents' abusive marriage, you have concluded that marriage is not good, your saboteur self will sabotage every relationship you ever have as soon as the M-word enters the conversation.

It's the same with money. If you believe that money has negative effects or that there's never enough, you will never be rich. Your saboteur self will make sure that you never exceed a certain level of income. It doesn't care about your conscious desire to become rich—its only concern is with being right.

Once again, though, as with the disowned self, your beliefs, attitudes, and prejudices tend to be buried in the subconscious mind, and for the most part, operate automatically and out of your conscious awareness. Nevertheless, if you watch how your life is working and observe what is showing up on a consistent basis, you can tell when your saboteur is operating—trying to be right according to the thought patterns buried in your subconscious mind.

So, taking the first of our two examples—the idea that "marriage is for the birds"—your saboteur self will ensure that, no matter how much you think you want to find a partner to marry, it will never happen. Everyone you meet will be in some way unavailable. Or you'll meet someone who is simply unable or unwilling to commit to a long-term relationship. If you get to, say, age forty, and this has been your experience, it doesn't take much to deduce that you have a thought pattern supported by your saboteur self that is strongly antithetical to the idea of marriage. At that point, you can have a heart-to-heart talk with your saboteur self about making some dramatic changes. In order to successfully adopt new ideas about marriage, such discussions and any subsequent changes must be done carefully and sensitively with regard to the subconscious mind's need to be right.

Nowhere is the saboteur more commonly operative than in the area of money. All of us have a financial "script." This is something we learned from an early age, and it determines the outlook of our entire financial life. Our saboteur sees to it that it does. Haven't you ever wondered why most people continue to earn more or less the same amount of money all their lives? Have you never asked yourself why some people are magnets for money and others always have to struggle to get by? It's not the outer circumstances of our lives that determine how much money we attract, but our internally integrated, subconscious financial script and the will of our saboteur self in ensuring that we adhere to that script.

Sometimes the saboteur is caught napping, and people experience an unusually high level of financial success—but only once. For instance, in performing a year-to-year review of people's financials, there is often a single but dramatic spike where, all of a sudden, a person will have a really good year. Almost invariably, though, this increase is followed by a dramatic drop the next year. From then on, the picture will revert to how it was before the spike and remain there for the foreseeable future. Anomalous financial increases of this nature cause our saboteur self, which was caught off guard by such a spike, to pay closer attention to our predetermined financial comfort zone and to prevent any such increases from sneaking through in the future. You should also know that we all have an income "set point." This is a point at the very top end of the comfort zone that sets our income ceiling and ensures we don't exceed it. It is part of our script.

When we have a fear of success, which a lot of people do, our saboteur is an expert at ensuring that success never happens. Fear of success is often formed when a child who is raised in a happy family observes that, as the father becomes increasingly successful at work, he is less and less available to give the kind of loving attention the child is used to. He or she notices that the mother is showing signs of being unhappy about that, too, and that the marriage is increasingly stressed as a result of the father being absent all the time. The child, therefore, begins to equate success with pain and suffering. If this was you, your saboteur will, in later life, allow success up to a certain level (comparable to the level where your father was before his rise to the next level began causing pain). But after that, if you were to get a big promotion, the saboteur would inevitably take action.

The saboteur self can strike in a variety of other ways: health problems that inhibit your ability to shine may suddenly occur; you may employ people beneath you who are incompetent; you may quarrel with your colleagues, upset your superiors, and make major mistakes; and so on. You will be lucky if you survive in that job. None of these events will be accidental. It'll be your saboteur at work.

Your saboteur self will most likely always be at odds with your ideal self for the reasons I have just listed and will, unfortunately, win most of the battles.

It will find all sorts of ways to divert you from your dreams, so you never become the person you most want to be. Try to be aware of the saboteur operating in your mind and put a stop to its subterfuge before it ruins everything.

Exercise #7: Identifying Your Saboteur Self

In your journal, plot a timeline of your life, starting from your early years to the present moment. See if you can observe patterns of behavior or experiences that might be indicative of beliefs or negative thought patterns so far prevalent in your life, and that your saboteur self has fought to defend and maintain. Some of these might be included in the following list. Check any you think might apply.

☐ "Life is inherently a struggle."

☐ "People are inherently bad."

☐ "All men are like my father."

☐ "All women are like my mother."

☐ "Rich people are crooks."

☐ "I cannot trust any man/woman."

☐ "I cannot trust life."

☐ "I can't trust anyone."

- [ ] "This is a dog-eat-dog world."
- [ ] "It's survival of the fittest."
- [ ] "I will always be discriminated against."
- [ ] "It is not OK for me to be powerful."
- [ ] "I am not worthy of anything."
- [ ] "I don't deserve . . ."
- [ ] "I am a failure."
- [ ] "I am not good at anything."
- [ ] "Everything I touch goes bad."
- [ ] "They just don't appreciate me."
- [ ] "I am invisible."
- [ ] "I am never paid well for what I do."
- [ ] "Even my own mother/father hates me."
- [ ] "I hate my mother/father."
- [ ] "I have to be perfect to get approval."
- [ ] "I have to be right."
- [ ] "There is never enough . . ."
- [ ] "To be loved, I have to be who I am not."
- [ ] "Others' needs are more important than my own."
- [ ] "I will never amount to anything."
- [ ] "If I become successful, I will be like my father."
- [ ] "You have to work hard for money."

☐ "Money does not grow on trees."

☐ "I have to struggle for money."

☐ "There is a shortage of money."

☐ "Money is a scarce commodity."

☐ "Money represents success."

☐ "Money is the root of all evil."

☐ "Other things are more important than money."

☐ "I should give money away."

☐ "Behind every fortune there is a great crime."

Once you have plotted your timeline and identified your thoughts and beliefs, you will have a better idea of what exactly your saboteur self is committed to defending.

THE SEXUAL SELF

This is an incredibly complex self. It is certainly worth delving into the sexual self in the interest of self-exploration and self-knowledge. It is also useful in helping us understand how we behave in relationships.

John Kappas, PhD, founder of the Hypnosis Motivation Institute and author of a number of books on hypnotherapy, developed a model of sexual personality that I find very helpful. It's called the Emotional & Physical Attraction model. On one side of the scale is the self that he describes as "physical sexual." On the other is a self described as "emotional sexual."

The terms *physical sexual* and *emotional sexual* can be misleading. What is being referred to here is how we *defend* the part of ourselves we feel to be most threatened. The physical sexual is driven by an intense fear of rejection. Feeling emotionally vulnerable, we defend our emotions by presenting our physical body at the forefront as a form of protection.

The emotional sexual, on the other hand, is driven by a strong fear of intimacy. Feeling vulnerable physically, we protect our body by constructing a wall of emotion, which contains feelings such as fear, intense shyness, and distrust. There are all sorts of ramifications for how each sexual personality shows up in the world. Following there is a scale that demonstrates the extremes of sexual personality to help you determine where on the continuum you might be. The ideal is to have no more than about a 60/40 bias toward one end or the other. This way you will be able to better understand those with the opposite bias.

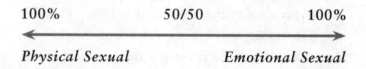

100%   50/50   100%

←——————————————————→

Physical Sexual   *Emotional Sexual*

People with a Physical Sexual Self

- They are classic extroverts who project their sexuality outward almost to the point of flaunting it.

- They are very comfortable with their bodies and have a high sex drive.

- They wear clothes and jewelry that emphasize and bring attention to their bodies and their sexual attractiveness.

- Image and appearance are very important to them. No matter what they buy, the main consideration is how it makes them look. They favor elegance, style, color, glitz, and so on. They would never buy a car on the basis of fuel efficiency over style.

- They crave acceptance and attention due to a fear of rejection, which means everything they do is for the purpose of receiving approval. As a result, they are extremely sensitive to criticism.

- When in conversation, they will stand close, lock eyes, and scan others' faces for the least sign of possible rejection.

- If rejected, rather than withdraw, they will push forward even more, trying to win others over with charm and persuasion. They become very insistent and pushy. They will not take "no" for an answer, especially from an emotional sexual person of the opposite sex to whom they are irresistibly attracted. They can be assertive and controlling, almost to the point of being obnoxious if they sense rejection.

- They are the life and soul of any party, very popular, and always seem comfortable in social situations. They are never at a loss for something to talk about, and small talk comes easily to them.

- They are natural risk-takers in all aspects of their lives. They are often entrepreneurs or indulge in very physical sports, especially team sports.

- They are less concerned about their bodies being hurt than they are about having their feelings crushed.

- All of their emotions are experienced physically rather than mentally, and when their feelings are hurt, they feel it as intense pain in their bodies. The pain can be so bad that it can literally incapacitate them for long periods of time.

- When a relationship ends, they are devastated and have a very difficult time letting go of it. They take it very personally and feel utterly rejected. They also have a very hard time replacing it. It may be many months before they will have another serious relationship, though they will have plenty of casual sex in the meanwhile. They need it just to feel OK.

- They are hopelessly idealistic about love and relationships and very romantically inclined. Once in a relationship, they tend to be loyal and monogamous. At the same time, they are very jealous and possessive.

- They enjoy children and are very connected to family (or the idea of family). They put family and relationships before career or any other aspect of life—it's their number one priority.

- They communicate by indirect implication and inferences, relying on the listener to make the correct interpretation. In contrast, they hear only what is said literally and don't pick up on implications. You have to tell them explicitly and frequently that you love them. They will not infer that you do just because you are there.

People with an Emotional Sexual Self

- They are the classic introverts, and they tend to withdraw into themselves to protect their feelings of physical vulnerability.
- They are not the least bit comfortable in their bodies and have a closed, protective bodily stance that says, "Don't come close, and don't touch me." Their arms will be in front of them as protection, and their feet tend to be turned inward when standing.
- They dress conservatively to divert attention away from their bodies and hide their sexuality, including full-coverage or baggy attire and sensible shoes. Women often wear minimal makeup, if any at all.
- They are not particularly social and have great difficulty making small talk. At parties, they are usually the wallflowers and they leave early.
- They feel their feelings inwardly and process them mentally. They seldom express feelings outwardly and do not like to show physical affection in public.
- They prefer not to be touched. Even the most innocent touch quickly results in some kind of irritation. The type of

touch that a physical sexual considers affectionate can seem like physical assault to an emotional sexual.

- They are turned on sexually much more by visual and mental stimuli than by touch.
- For them, sex is not a high priority; neither is family, children, or relationships. Their priority is work and career, followed by their hobbies. Relationships come a distant third. They are not very fond of children, and they may choose never to marry.
- They often have extramarital affairs and think little of it, because they do not equate love with sex as do their physical sexual counterparts. They enjoy the mental excitement of affairs.
- When a relationship ends, they get over it in a matter of days and replace it easily. They do not take breakups as a personal rejection.
- They don't generally like team sports, but they do excel at individual sports that require rigorous training and personal challenges.
- They lead with their minds in everything, from work, to games, and even sex. They are analytical, careful, and methodical and, therefore, seldom spontaneous.

- They buy cars based not on style and image but based on which are the most efficient and best engineered. They will research such purchases extensively before they buy.
- If they go into business for themselves, they tend to be accountants, computer programmers, engineers, researchers, or technicians. They like precise, solitary work and are detail oriented. They can be very successful in business.
- They pick up on inferences and subtle implications, but they speak very directly and precisely. They don't waste words and are not physically expressive.

I can't conclude this conversation on the sexual self without explaining how this dynamic plays out in relationships, especially if one or both partners are at an extreme end of the scale. As you might imagine, opposites attract—initially. A high physical sexual will attract a high emotional sexual, and vice versa. At a party, a high physical sexual male will make a beeline for the retiring little emotional sexual who is in the corner clutching her drink and looking shy and embarrassed. He desperately wants to rescue her and "bring her out." She is initially turned off by him because he's so pushy, but eventually succumbs to his irresistible charm and his "take charge" attitude.

Communication seems to flow easily between them, as well. That's because the physical sexual speaks inferentially to the emotional sexual, who easily picks up on the subtle implications of what is being said. Conversely, the emotional sexual speaks directly to the physical sexual, who likes direct communication, not implications. The emotional sexual says little, but is a good listener, whereas the physical sexual loves to dominate the conversation and is more than happy to have someone who will just listen. It seems like a match made in heaven. Not only does the communication seem great, but during the honeymoon period, which lasts about six months, the emotional sexual tends to act like a physical sexual in bed. So everything seems wonderful and the physical sexual is convinced that he or she has found a soul mate. However, at around six months, they begin reverting to their natural type. As the chemistry that enabled them to let down their defenses for a while begins to fade, so, too, do their defenses reemerge, and their primary behavior returns to the forefront.

Consequently, emotional sexuals begin withdrawing emotionally and wanting less sex. Their fear of intimacy and their tendency to avoid it returns. They begin focusing on things that interest them besides the relationship. This drives the physical sexual crazy because he or she interprets the emotional sexual's behavior as implicit rejection and an indication of the partner falling out of love. That makes him or her even more demanding of love, sex, and physical affection, which in turn makes the emotional sexual withdraw even more.

Once both fear responses have kicked in, the situation goes from bad to worse, and the relationship is virtually irretrievable. If they stay together, it will be the emotional sexual who controls the relationship. That's because the physical sexual will sell a large chunk of himself or herself (remember lost selves?) in order to get whatever sex or physical affection the emotional sexual is willing to give. That's why a lot of strong-looking physical sexual males are controlled by weaker-looking wives. A woman who knows how to manipulate that fear of rejection owns her man.

You might imagine that the ideal arrangement would be two of the same type together. This is not so. Two physical sexuals together would be in competition with each other and would act like a couple of divas. They would talk at each other in implications, with neither of them fully understanding the meaning. They would talk over each other and always see rejection in every utterance. It would be an intensely sexual liaison, but their jealousy and possessiveness would create terrible problems. They would always be fighting.

Two emotional sexuals together would soon get very bored with one another. Sex would be nonexistent, and their communication minimal. Their best chance at survival would be if they were to work together. Otherwise, one or both would likely be out looking for an affair just to relieve the boredom.

Concluding this discussion on the sexual self, I would ask you to please remember that these are the extremes. Most of us are either predominantly physical or emotional, but have enough of the other to find balance to a greater or lesser degree. You can probably make a rough assessment of where you are on that scale, which can give you a sufficient idea of your sexual self. Again, you will want to compare this assessment with your authentic self to ensure that there is congruence.

4 Working with Guilt and Shame

THE TWO EMOTIONS MOST CLOSELY associated with self-forgiveness and self-acceptance are guilt and shame. It behooves us, therefore, to study these two emotions in order to understand how they differ and how they interact.

We can define guilt as a feeling of remorse over something that we have done but should not have, or on the contrary, not done but should have. It's about our behavior.

Shame is different from guilt in the sense that shame is remorse, not so much over what we have done or not done, but about the kind of person we think we are or should be. Obviously, there is a relationship between them in that our guilt over what we have done might lead us to feeling a sense of shame about ourselves, but making a distinction between guilt and shame is important to the Radical Self-Forgiveness process.

Acknowledging this distinction is an essential part of understanding self-forgiveness and self-acceptance. Self-forgiveness is a process that enables us to release guilt, while self-acceptance is a process that enables us to process our shame. Graphically, we can see the interrelatedness of the two concepts, as shown in figure 2.

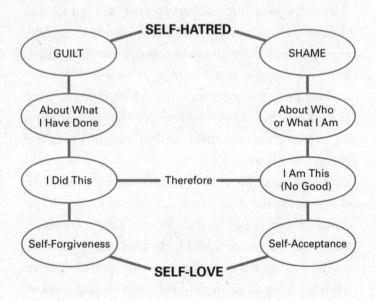

FIGURE 2   Guilt vs. Shame

Though there are obviously strong connections between self-forgiveness and self-acceptance, as indicated by the line linking "I did this" to "I am this (no good)," the two are unique because they generate distinct emotional responses. The "I did this, therefore I am this (no good)" loop adds to whatever shame is already there. In the end, though, it all adds up to emotional pain—the pain of separation within oneself.

GUILT

If we were unable to experience feelings of guilt, we would be just as crippled as someone who was unable to feel fear. Whereas a truly fearless person would never be able to sense or evaluate danger or risk, a person without the capacity to feel guilt would be an amoral sociopath, unable to gauge how to act in the world relative to the understood rules of the game.

One of the ways we evaluate child development is how well developed the child's sense of moral judgment has become by a certain age. Jean Piaget, the Swiss child psychologist, declared it to be a stage of development that a child must master if he or she is to develop to maturity. Moral judgment depends on the capacity to feel and to anticipate guilt. Without

83

guilt, we would not know how to calibrate our behavior toward others so as not to insult them or injure them in some other way. Guilt is an internal compass that guides us to do what is right, and to the extent that we make good judgments in this direction, it gives us a strong sense of self-worth and personal integrity. If we had no ability to feel guilt or shame, we would not know whether we acted out of integrity or not. Values and principles would mean nothing to us, so we would never know how to act appropriately in any given situation.

Acknowledging that we have a complex set of agreements about how we should behave toward one another, all other forms of life, our planet, and so on is part of being human. We refer to these agreements as our *code of ethics*. Ethics make an appeal to our principles and values and to our personal sense of integrity. For example, if we declare our belief in a principle like loyalty or fidelity, and then act in such a way as to contravene that principle, we are not acting out of integrity. To be in integrity means being whole, so whenever we compromise our integrity, we fracture our self-worth and lose a vital part of ourselves.

Ethics tend to change little over the years, although each culture has its own code of ethics and prioritization of values. America's primary value is freedom of the individual, often at the cost of most other values. Other advanced societies, such as in the Scandavian countries and most of Europe and Great Britain, tend to value the common good over the individual. Neither set of values is right or wrong. The dominance of particular values is a function of how each individual culture has evolved over hundreds of years. For example, in Western civilization, many principles that we hold dear, such as freedom of speech, respect for persons, equality of opportunity, and so on, stem from ancient times.

Morals are different from ethics in that they don't necessarily reference deeply held principles—they are merely social agreements (or disagreements) about what is considered "right" and what is "wrong" in our current time. These social agreements are established according to the prevailing moral code of the day, much of which is formed not so much by rational thought as by attitudes, prejudices, habits of mind, peer pressure, media pressure, and so on. As we've seen many times throughout history, morals can change very quickly, especially from one generation to the next.

A good example of how quickly a moral code can change is our perspective on homosexuality.

Just think about how our opinions of homosexuality have evolved over the last twenty to thirty years. In the 1970s and 1980s, homosexuals were rejected as completely immoral and unacceptable. Although there is still some significant religious fervor against homosexuality, it is now much more commonly accepted in many places throughout the world. A measure of how dramatically attitudes have changed can be most prominently seen in the fight to allow homosexuals to marry.

With regard to religion, some argue that it is impossible to be a moral person without having a religion to guide one's moral code. While this may be true for some people by choice, this does not mean it is true for everyone. In fact, to be told that one's moral code depends on religious conviction can be insulting, since we are quite capable, if we so choose, of calibrating our moral code according to ethical principles without reference to religious or dogmatic rules given to us by some outside authority. Atheists are equally capable of being moral and ethical as those who subscribe to particular religions.

Whether your moral compass is formed by the prevailing culture, parental guidance, or religious dogma is essentially irrelevant. The important thing is to have one and to believe in it. You need morals to guide your conscience. To have a conscience, you must have a well-developed sense of anticipatory guilt. A fully developed conscience is wrought from the personal experience of grappling with principle—not by referencing some kind of rule book.

Anticipatory guilt serves as our internal ethical and moral compass and, hopefully, prevents us from going ahead with something that would break a commonly held agreement on what is generally considered to be the right thing to do. It is a "guilt avoidance system." When tempted to act in a way that would be against the legal or moral code of the day, our conscience causes us to consider how we might feel about it afterward. Then, based upon the amount of guilt we think we might feel, we either proceed with the act or we don't. For many, the guilt would simply be too much to bear.

Such tests to moral code come into play on a daily basis for each and every one of us. For example, if a sales assistant in a store gave us too much change, it would be our conscience that would quickly assess whether the amount of guilt we felt outweighed the initial temptation to pocket the extra cash and say nothing. A more serious example would be the temptation to cheat on one's spouse. Such a temptation could be great, and anticipating the potential pleasure could be enormously enjoyable. However, if we believe in the principles of fidelity and honor, our anticipatory guilt meter should kick in immediately. It will then be a battle between two conflicting principles—personal freedom and fidelity to one's partner. Conflicts of this nature are ultimately resolved by being processed through one's conscience.

We also have moral rules, many of which are actually laws, about how people are held accountable for breaking such commitments. These rules are interpreted and institutionally administered in reference to a socially agreed upon code of justice. However, even if no law is broken, certain transgressions are considered such serious breaches of the moral code that society itself exacts its own form of punishment. Punishment of this nature can take the form of subtle or not-so-subtle discrimination, ostracizing, career impairment, media condemnation, and so on. Needless to say, social reactions can be severe.

Retrospective guilt is the guilt that we feel after we have done something "wrong." There's no recovering from it—the deed is done—apologies notwithstanding. And in any case, apologies are to help the other person feel better, not to lessen our own guilt. However, we are still in a position to decide whether or not the guilt exists and whether it is appropriate or inappropriate. As we have seen, the judging self makes no distinction between appropriate and inappropriate guilt, but if we find our guilt to be inappropriate, we can launch a legitimate challenge to the barrage of criticism coming from the judge. So what is the difference between appropriate and inappropriate guilt?

Appropriate Retrospective Guilt

If we have broken an agreement, we *should* feel guilty. For example, if we got drunk, drove recklessly, and killed someone, we are entitled to feel guilty about it. We behaved badly, which resulted in fatal consequences. Our guilt is appropriate. It is rightfully there to be felt. We are entitled to it. This guilt is our way of owning our responsibility and administering a form of self-justice. Our guilt is evidence that we have a well-formed conscience. In this case, guilt is our teacher.

Inappropriate Retrospective Guilt

On the other hand, if we were driving safely and a cyclist swerved in front of us, such that we had no way to avoid him or stop, and we killed him, guilt would be inappropriate under such circumstances. It's totally reasonable to feel sad and full of regret, of course, but not guilty. This situation doesn't warrant feelings of guilt—we would not be entitled to it, and we must tell our judging self so. We would need to do this because, without doubt, the judging self would have seized the opportunity and would have been shrill in its condemnation of us within seconds of the event, notwithstanding the fact that we were in no way to blame.

Inappropriate guilt, then, is felt when we blame ourselves for something that we did not consciously choose, had no control over, no responsibility for, and for which we cannot reasonably be held accountable. You often hear people say things like, "Yes, but if only I had done this or that. . . ." or, "I should have done this. . . ." when clearly there was no apparent reason for them to have foreseen the need to do any such thing prior to the event.

Survivor's guilt is a form of inappropriate guilt. It occurs when, for example, a group of people die in a fire, and a survivor feels guilty for making it out alive. Military people suffer this form of guilt a great deal when they survive a campaign that has killed their comrades in arms. The question always arises: why me?

Inferred guilt occurs when we feel guilty by infer-
ence. We understand from others that they think we
are to blame, and even though we are innocent, we feel
guilty—especially when we are around them. This is
a codependent emotion, and it is completely inappropriate. Nevertheless, it is hard to ignore those
inferences, especially in cases where society as a
whole is suggesting we are guilty.

Guilt by association arises when we feel guilty for
the actions of those connected with us. Parents who
feel guilty for what their children have done is one
prevalent example. Again, this is codependency. (In
some cases, however, they may be entitled to feel
appropriate guilt for not being good parents.)

Projected guilt is especially precarious—don't
buy in to it! This happens when other people feel
guilty themselves, and rather than feel it, they project it onto us. Such projections are often filled with
an incredible amount of blame and guilt trips galore.
Once again, if we are codependent, we might fall for
it, but it is, of course, inappropriate guilt.

Exercise #8: How Entitled Are You to Your Guilt?
The distinctions to be made between appropriate
and inappropriate guilt are often subtle and not
always easy to make. But honing our ability to

recognize and process these forms of guilt is worthwhile and can lead to an immediate reduction in the amount of guilt that we feel.

Make a list of all the things you either feel guilty about now or have felt guilty about in the past. On a scale of 1–10, assess your overall level of guilt. Then assess how much of your guilt is appropriate or inappropriate. Any that comes in the category of associated, projected, or inferred should be included in the "inappropriate" column.

EVENT	OVERALL GUILT SCORE	% APPR.	% INAPPR.
_____	_____	_____	_____
_____	_____	_____	_____
_____	_____	_____	_____
_____	_____	_____	_____
_____	_____	_____	_____
_____	_____	_____	_____
_____	_____	_____	_____
_____	_____	_____	_____
_____	_____	_____	_____
_____	_____	_____	_____

Expressed as a percentage, to what degree has your guilt been reduced simply as a result of completing this exercise?

SHAME

Whereas guilt is remorse over something we have done, shame is remorse over who we think we are as a human being. To be shamed is to be made to feel worthless, bad, undeserving, less than, and simply no good. The result of being consistently and severely shamed is a feeling of considerable self-loathing.

As we discussed in the introduction, self-loathing is surprisingly common. It can range from a vague feeling of questionable self-worth, to severe self-hatred expressed in a number of extreme ways, such as self-mutilation and other forms of self-punishment or even suicide. Clearly, there is a strong relationship between guilt and shame, and much of what I've presented in the preceding pages will be equally applicable to shame. The judging self, for example, is not only shrill in telling us *what* we have done wrong, it will also lose no time in suggesting that *we* are wrong.

The saboteur self is also always looking for opportunities to create problems for us by defending some of our shame-based, core negative beliefs about ourselves, such as, "I am worthless," "I am bad," "I am no good," and so on. Beliefs like these then become the basis for new, more complex beliefs, such as:

"I am worthless, so people will never value me or see me as being important or worth listening to."

"I am bad, so no one will ever want me, and I will always be alone."

"I am no good, so I don't deserve to have much in life."

"I am not enough for anyone, so people will always leave me when they find out who I really am."

How Toxic Is a Belief Based on Shame?

Very toxic! In fact, it can even kill you. Psychotherapist, author, and researcher Lawrence LeShan has spent a lifetime working with cancer patients, studying how the mind-body connection impacts the incidence of cancer. In his book *Cancer as a Turning Point*, he revealed his discovery of an underlying, unconscious belief common to virtually every cancer patient with whom he ever worked: "If I show up as who I am (bad, horrible, ugly, worthless, stupid, and so on) no one will love me; therefore, in order to be loved, I have to pretend to be someone I am not."

According to O. Carl Simonton in his book *The Cancer Personality*, many people who get cancer tend to be "nice" people. This often means that they have spent their lives being people pleasers—always molding themselves according to the desires and preferences of others, always prioritizing others' needs over their own, providing caretaking, avoiding conflict, and doing whatever necessary to achieve their desired level of acceptance. In other words, these people have spent their lives specializing in being who they are *not* in order to receive love and approval. In reality, they have sold themselves out. But the worst of it is, in spite of everything, deep down their belief that they are unlovable remains.

Not surprisingly then, deep inside of them is seething rage and resentment. They are mad at whomever it was that caused them to feel this way. They are mad at themselves for believing that they are unlovable and selling out just to get approval. But the problem is that beliefs like this are so deeply repressed that the people have no idea that they are there, and of course, they never show. As you might expect, this kind of repressed energy (in the form of anger, resentment, and rage) has to come out somewhere, so it eventually shows up as a condition in the physical body. Even if your toxic negative belief doesn't kill you, it will almost certainly cause you to live an impoverished, limited, insecure, and perhaps even loveless life.

There are five steps in the process of transforming these core negative beliefs. These are:

1. Discover
2. Recognize
3. Evaluate
4. Neutralize
5. Transform

The remainder of this chapter considers each of these steps in turn.

STEP 1: DISCOVER THE BELIEFS

If you are paying any attention at all to your judging self, you may be aware of these beliefs already, playing them over and over inside your head every day. The judging self might use code words for the beliefs, but with a little bit of critical listening and acting as the observer in this case, you might begin to uncover the basic negative beliefs that fuel your constant tirade of self-judgment.

For beliefs that are more deeply buried in the subconscious mind, we might have to do some real detective work to uncover them completely. Such a process would be extremely difficult but for the fact that your judging self and saboteur self will always conspire to display these beliefs as correct by ensuring that they come to fruition in your life as if they were really true. These beliefs actually create your reality.

Although this playing-out of beliefs can make life quite miserable for you if left as is, it actually works to your advantage when it comes to discovering what your true beliefs are. You can infer what your subconscious beliefs are from what is showing up in your life. Life will always mirror your beliefs for you, no matter what they are. Here are some examples:

Observation: I don't have much of anything in my life.
Likely Belief: I am not deserving of nor worthy of it.

Observation: I always seem to screw things up.
Likely Belief: I can never do it right.

Observation: I have always had to work hard to survive.
Likely Belief: I always have to struggle in life.

Also, through the Law of Attraction, you will attract people into your life who will treat you exactly in accordance with these beliefs. This helps even more in discovering what they are. For example:

Observation: People seem not to notice me.
Likely Belief: I am invisible.

Observation: People don't listen to me.
Likely Belief: I have nothing worthwhile to say.

Observation: People are always trying to change me.
Likely Belief: I am not OK the way I am.

Observation: My relationships never last long.
Likely Belief: I am unlovable.

Exercise #9: Identifying Your Shame-Based Core Negative Beliefs

Take a look at the following list of beliefs and check the ones you think might be buried within you, based upon your life experiences up until this point.

☐ "I have to be perfect to be loved."
☐ "If I show up as me, no one will love me."

- ☐ "I have to struggle/work hard for everything."
- ☐ "I never quite measure up."
- ☐ "I don't deserve love."
- ☐ "Others are more important than me."
- ☐ "I don't matter."
- ☐ "I can never do it right."
- ☐ "I always do it wrong."
- ☐ "I am not worthy of love."
- ☐ "I don't deserve _____."
- ☐ "I'll never make it on my own."
- ☐ "My life has no real value."
- ☐ "I'm always left out of everything."
- ☐ "I can't trust anyone."
- ☐ "I am invisible and hardly ever noticed."
- ☐ "I'm all alone in the world."
- ☐ "I am not worthy of money or riches."
- ☐ "To be loved, I need to be sick."
- ☐ "I'll never be good enough."
- ☐ "I never finish anything."
- ☐ "I'm too rebellious."
- ☐ "There is never enough _____ for me."
- ☐ "Something must be wrong with me."

☐ "I have to stay in control."
☐ "I'll never have enough money."
☐ "I'll never be a success."
☐ "Bad things always happen to me."
☐ "I can't have what I really want."
☐ "I'm just not lovable the way I am."
☐ "I will always fail at everything."
☐ "I'm too distracted."
☐ "If I open my heart, I'll get hurt."
☐ "I am not likeable."
☐ "It's not safe to be me."
☐ "I am a failure."
☐ "I shouldn't even have been born."
☐ "If I tell the truth, they will leave."
☐ "My feelings are not important."
☐ "I create my own (bad) reality."
☐ "I am spiritually flawed."
☐ "I am not smart enough."
☐ "I am intimidating to others."
☐ _____
☐ _____
☐ _____

STEP 2: RECOGNIZE THE BELIEFS

Your judging self didn't just make these beliefs up. They came from somewhere, or more accurately, from someone. Somebody shamed you into thinking you were precisely what you now believe yourself to be.

Whose voice was it that convinced you that you were not OK? Since we can fairly say that most of our beliefs about ourselves are established in our earliest years, it follows that, for most of us at least, it was our parents who were our primary influences in this regard. By and large, they taught us everything we know about ourselves through what they said—or didn't say—to us or about us; what they did—or didn't do—to us and for us; and by how they reacted to us whenever we ventured to express our true nature.

It is a role that falls naturally upon parents—they have no choice in the matter. (If you are a parent, you know this for yourself. It is simply thrust upon you.) Neither do parents have training in, nor even in many cases an awareness of, that awesome responsibility that begins to weigh heavily even before birth. They can do no more than stumble along, doing the best they can with little knowledge, scant experience, and the most meager set of tools to assist them in nurturing an emerging human being.

We must remember, too, that just like everyone else, most parents are wounded human beings themselves. Like everyone else, they have a tendency to project their pain onto others—most often onto those they love—particularly those they can influence the most and over whom they have power and control, such as their children. Parents also have no choice but to pass on their own values and morals, codes of behavior, skills, attitudes, prejudices, dreams, thought habits, and so on to their children. It's impossible not to do that—it's what parents must do.

Taking all this into account, it is hardly surprising that most of us inferred, from the way our parents carried out this role, that we were somehow not OK. We surmised that we were flawed in some particular way or that we should not expect to be successful, rich, powerful, or deserving. Research shows that even in what we might judge as "nice" homes, children grow up hearing about twenty negative messages about themselves for every one positive message. Add to this the fact that the most frequently used and most damaging form of punishment used by most parents—especially in middle-class families—is the prolonged withholding of love, and you begin to understand why so many people feel that they are not lovable.

In the beginning of this section, I said that our parents taught us what to think about ourselves. That is not exactly true. Other than those of us who clearly were cruelly and intentionally shamed by our parents, most of us inferred from our parents' words and behavior what kind of a person we were and would become—and for the most part, we were dead wrong.

Why Our Beliefs Are Almost Always Wrong

Chapter 1 in my book *Radical Forgiveness* tells the true story about how my sister, Jill, came to feel *not enough* by initially inferring from our father that, because he wasn't demonstrative toward her (not bouncing her on his knee, for example), he did not love her. That was untrue, but that was her perception at the time.

She then extrapolated from that original interpretation that if her own father couldn't/wouldn't/didn't love her, then she wasn't enough for him. Therefore, she wouldn't ever be enough for *any* man. This became her core negative belief. She recreated that story in her life over and over. Just as her last marriage was about to break up, she was finally able to see how her husband was reflecting that belief back to her by treating her as if she were indeed not enough.

This is typical of how we erroneously infer what kind of a person we are from how people treat us. If we get beaten every day, we conclude that we are deserving of it and must be deeply flawed. We typically carry such a belief to our grave because we fail to see that the man or woman who beat us was deeply wounded and flawed, and that it was not about us. It was about him or her. That said, if you feel that you need to do some forgiveness work around your parents for treating you badly and for making you feel less than OK, then by all means use the Radical Forgiveness Worksheet for this purpose. You can easily download this worksheet from soundstrue.com/radicalforgiveness.

STEP 3: EVALUATE THE BELIEFS

This step requires some honesty and courage to face the fact that, while most of the beliefs may well be false, some of the flaws others criticize and even punish you for may have an element of truth about them. If that is the case, it is vital that you own them and accept them—even if they are not pretty.

For example, perhaps you were criticized for being lazy, lacking ambition, or being untidy; being antisocial, stingy, or too sensitive; or for not being sporty enough, smart enough, and so on. Maybe you are still being criticized for these things even today. Well, the fact is, that could just be the kind of person you are and were. It's just how you were made.

Take a few moments to review the list of qualities you recognized as belonging to your authentic self and see whether these qualities for which you were shamed are, in fact, part of your authentic self. The important thing to understand is that the problem belongs to the people doing the judging, *not* you. It's not your problem—it's their problem. If they don't like it, you could easily and justifiably tell them to go take a hike! But in your early years, you couldn't contradict your mother or father, older brother or sister, or even your teachers and priests. Besides, you thought they were always right, so you took what they said about you as true and felt that it was not OK to be the real you.

Exercise #10: True/False Core Negative Beliefs

Go back over the list of core negative beliefs in Exercise #9 and select the ones that reflect the underlying judgments made about you by your parents and others. For example, your core negative beliefs might indicate that you are untidy, never satisfied, indecisive, antisocial, unintelligent, undisciplined, too sensitive, not manly enough, always complaining, too bookish, too academic, never able to sit still, rebellious, wild, seductive, secretive, nosey, and so on. List these traits in the following table.

Which of them would you lay claim to as being either true or at least partially true as an honest description of how you are now? Give each one a rating on a scale of 0–100 of how much truth it holds, where 100 = 100% true.

BELIEFS	% TRUE

STEP 4: NEUTRALIZE THE BELIEFS

The only way to neutralize core negative beliefs is to stop giving them energy. One way to do this is to turn them around so that you are able to recognize what you were previously criticized for in a more positive light. For example, if you were criticized for being undisciplined, perhaps it could be seen as evidence of your creative mind and your ability to think laterally and outside the box. By taking a new approach, you diffuse the charge of the original criticism and thereby neutralize the shame-based belief.

Recasting the negative quality as a positive attribute is not the same thing as making an affirmation. An affirmation is simply a statement, usually in opposition to a negative belief, affirming that you believe the positive, even though you don't. The hope is that if you say it often enough it will override the negative belief. It never does.

Affirmations are very weak because they reside in your conscious mind and are, in effect, just another form of denial. The negative belief that you are trying to eliminate with your affirmation is fully alive in the subconscious mind and is many times more powerful than the affirmation, and it never gives way easily. When the chips are down and the belief gets activated, it will simply brush the affirmation aside.

Exercise #11: Making the Negative Positive

Identify which of your core negative beliefs might be recast in a positive light. For each one, attempt a positive reinterpretation. Here are some examples:

> "I seem untidy because I am not a visual person. I am more kinesthetic and identify more with how I feel. My comfort is what matters to me, not how things look."

> "I may seem antisocial; however, I like my own company and prefer to choose my company carefully."

> "I may look undisciplined and scatterbrained, but in fact I am creative and able to do lots of things at the same time—it's multitasking, and it's a valuable talent."

> "I was told I was nosey, but I am simply inquisitive and curious about things, which shows a healthy mind."

Note in the space provided the beliefs you feel you could work on recasting in a positive light.

_____

_____

_____

_____

_____

_____

_____

_____

_____

_____

_____

_____

_____

_____

_____

_____

STEP 5: TRANSFORM THE BELIEFS

Suppose that what you are being criticized for has no redeeming quality, at least nothing that you can see. Suppose you really are dishonest, mean, or cruel. Could you accept any one of those things about yourself, too? That's more difficult, is it not?

The only way to fully transform these beliefs is not by trying to eliminate them or modify them, but by accepting them just the way they are. This is not the work of the ego—it can only be achieved through the services of that part of our psyche known as our Spiritual Intelligence. This is the part of us that knows the truth of who we are, why we have taken on these beliefs, and what value they bring to our spiritual growth. It is also the part of us that is connected to Universal Intelligence.

We activate our Spiritual Intelligence by using the worksheets and other tools provided by the Radical Forgiveness technology. In this case, it would be the Radical Self-Acceptance Worksheet. It is only by using one of these tools that the transformation can occur. We'll visit the Radical Self-Acceptance Worksheet in Chapter 10. Meanwhile, let's begin the process with the following exercise.

Exercise #12: This Is Who I Am

In your journal or on a separate piece of paper, write a lighthearted but confident description of precisely who you are today, making clear all your attributes—both positive and negative. You have reclaimed parts of you that you had previously disowned, accepted parts of you that you didn't much like and were judged for, retrieved parts you had given away or traded, and released the parts that were created just to please others. Make it a celebration of your uniqueness and of your newfound wholeness. Make it a statement that says, "Here I am!" You might even finish it off with a statement like, "And if you don't like it, that's your problem."

DEFINING YOUR BELIEFS

We have spent the previous chapters exploring the nature of self and, in particular, how you show up in the world as *you*. The previous section of this chapter ended with the invitation to make a broad proclamation about who you are. This section invites you to respond to the question "What do I believe?"

You have probably realized by now that traditional forgiveness and Radical Forgiveness spring from two very different worldviews. Knowing how your beliefs fit within this discussion will help you determine whether you are going to stop at traditional self-forgiveness or be willing to persevere to achieve Radical Self-Forgiveness and Self-Acceptance. At this point, I want to remind you that the process of Radical Forgiveness does not require that you believe in it. This means that you don't have to actually change your worldview for it to work. All it requires is your willingness to at least be a tiny bit open to some of the ideas contained in the new paradigm and to see whether or not it works when you use the tools provided. Additionally, it will be interesting to see if your worldview changes as a result of doing the work.

That doesn't mean that what we have done up to now cannot be used to alleviate any guilt and shame you might have been holding on to. Just knowing the difference between appropriate and inappropriate guilt and being aware of the five steps to releasing negative beliefs about yourself will be extremely useful.

The worldview that prevails today is based on a whole set of beliefs derived from our ability to process our experiences in the physical world through our five senses. We automatically believe what we see, hear, feel, smell, and taste. We refine these beliefs by taking measurements and studying all the phenomena available in order to make all sorts of scientific deductions about them and life in general. But we draw the line at the point where objectivity is questioned. Subjective experience—our multisensory awareness of our internal landscape and how that intersects with outer reality—is not given much, if any, consideration.

Another, much older paradigm, which runs parallel to, and in many ways includes the prevailing one, says that there is a lot more to life than our five-sensory reality suggests. We refer to this expanded view of reality as a metaphysical worldview. Generally speaking, this paradigm asks us to look beyond the physical descriptions of reality and to entertain the possibility that reality has a large, unseen spiritual element to it that comes to us in the form of subjective, multi-sensory experience, and that this element plays a big part in our lives. For some people, this spiritual element is experienced through some form of religion grounded in the idea of there being one God who gives life to everything.

Christianity has always had its own metaphysical or mystical tradition, especially within the Catholic church. Jesus was metaphysical in his teachings. Meanwhile, the Kabbalah provides the mystical underpinning of Judaism, and the religions of the East have always been metaphysical in their outlook. For those with a more secular/spiritual viewpoint, the paradigm is experienced as some mysterious power or intelligence that, while it includes us, is greater than our individual selves. Many Europeans, having largely given up on organized religion, are of this mind. Nevertheless, people of this persuasion as well as those who conceptualize a God would hold that a spiritual element intervenes in their lives in dramatic ways and cannot be dismissed as mere superstition. The word I use to describe that intervention is *grace*, and as an example of how grace works in our lives, there is none better than Radical Forgiveness.

Anne Lamott, in her wonderful book *Grace (Eventually)*, says that there are only two prayers—"help" and "thank you." Radical Forgiveness is a form of secular prayer in which we are simply asking for help in seeing the divine perfection in a particular situation, and expressing our gratitude for that gift and for the intervention that always seems to follow.

Exercise #13: Identifying What You Believe

Take a look at the following paradigms, and give each one a rating between 0 and 100 percent according to how closely it adheres to your own. You will probably find that you identify with elements from more than one, so you may benefit from drafting a composite sample, using elements from each, that more accurately describes your own personal worldview.

I should stress that none of these is better than any other, nor is any one of them an impediment to having success with Radical Self-Forgiveness or Radical Self-Acceptance. They are simply offered as another way to learn about your own self in the interest of self-knowledge. That said, these paradigms may show you where you could encounter some resistance to the ideas presented in part two of this book. If you do experience resistence, simply ignore the ideas that don't fit your paradigm and use the technology with as much skepticism as you wish. The important thing is not to let your ideas get in the way of attempting to see if the technology works—it always does.

Paradigm 1

I take a rather scientific/secular/rational view of life. I think that human beings are simply part of the evolutionary spiral and that, like every other animal on the planet, we are born, we live, and then we die. Yes, there's a lot more to it, but that's more or less it in a nutshell. I am not a strong believer in a deity (God), though I wouldn't go so far as to call myself an atheist. I am not inclined to think there is a reality beyond what I register with my five senses. If there is, I have no real idea what that might be like. I am certainly not in touch with it and wouldn't know how to talk about it. Until now, forgiveness to me has meant making a conscious decision to let bygones be bygones.

Rating: _____%

Paradigm 2

My spirituality and worldview come directly from my religious beliefs. I tend to see the world as a continuous struggle between good and evil. I believe that evil (Satan) does exist, and it is my job to stay vigilant and defend against the ever-present danger of it coming into my life. God made this world, and He made me as well. He remains in heaven but is always watching and judging me harshly for having committed the original sin. When I die, I hope He will judge me kindly, though, and I will go to heaven. If I don't live a good life, I will go to hell. I believe in being kind to others, but I believe forgiveness is not ours to bestow. All we can do is ask God (or Jesus) to do it on our behalf. So, in my opinion, forgiveness is prayer, and ultimately, should the prayer be answered, it is pure grace.

Rating: _____%

Paradigm 3

I am somewhat open to spiritual ideas and find them intellectually interesting, but I wouldn't necessarily call myself a very spiritual person. I am somewhat open to the idea that we are here to learn certain lessons, and I do try to interpret life in this way, but I don't find it easy in practice. Even though I am quick to blame and see fault in others, I try to entertain the possibility that the person I am upset with is there to teach me something. I know I shouldn't try to figure out what the lesson is, but I am an intellectual person and love to know the how and why of things. I also understand at the intellectual level that others are providing an opportunity to learn and grow, but I find it hard to really integrate that belief into my being—I always struggle with that in real life. I understand at the intellectual level that true forgiveness comes when we realize that everything happens for a reason, but in everyday life I find that difficult to put into practice.

Rating: _____%

Paradigm 4

I see life as a mystery, not so much to be understood and figured out, but to be experienced as fully as possible. I think the most spiritual people are the ones who exhibit the most humanness. I am open to the idea that there is more than one reality. There is at least this physical reality that we inhabit bodily every day, but I am also open to the idea that there is another reality that we cannot see, which we might call the spiritual reality. I don't think anyone really knows what that reality is, but when I open my eyes fully and feel into my gut, I sense enough evidence that such a reality exists. I am comfortable with that. I have my own way of connecting with that reality and expressing my spirituality (organized religion, being a member of like-minded groups, meditation, retreats, healing, praying, chanting, and so on), and I am happy with this. Forgiveness, to me, is done by extending compassion to others and seeing them as imperfect human beings just like me and everyone else.

Rating: _____%

Paradigm 5

I am a spiritual being having a human experience. By that I mean that I have chosen to come to Earth in order to learn lessons and evolve spiritually. This is the school, and life is the curriculum. What happens during my life are my individual lessons. I have come into the life experience with the desire to fully grasp what oneness is by experiencing the opposite of it—separation. I made agreements with other souls prior to my incarnation that they would do things not so much to me—though it will feel that way while I am in a body—but for me. While I'm here, I also enroll others to give me opportunities to learn. They look like my enemies, but I see them as my healing angels. That's how I see forgiveness—that everything that happens invariably occurs for a spiritual purpose and that, while I remain accountable for what I do in the human world, in purely spiritual terms nothing wrong ever happens.

Rating: _____%

Paradigm 6

I am totally into metaphysics, and I see myself as a very spiritual person. I see our life on this planet as being on the wheel of karma, reincarnating over and over, lifetime after lifetime, learning lessons, balancing energies, and evolving spiritually until one reaches completion. I am in touch with the spiritual realm and receive guidance from that side of the veil. I have several spirit guides, and I frequently talk with angels. I believe that we human beings are all part of the Godhead—our purpose for our lives being to assist God in expanding His/Her consciousness and to eventually co-create heaven on earth. As far as forgiveness is concerned, I am certain in my own mind that everything is in perfect divine order and that there is nothing to forgive. Forgiveness, therefore, is moot.

Rating: _____%

Now write your own personal worldview below to complete this exercise.

_____

_____

_____

_____

_____

_____

_____

_____

_____

_____

_____

This exercise may have seemed somewhat academic and perhaps even a bit redundant, but I think you will find it to have been very instructive with regard to how the process of Radical Forgiveness and Radical Self-Forgiveness proceeds through five specific stages as outlined in the next chapter. In particular, you will find the value in having done the exercise when you come to examine the fourth stage: Reframing the Story.

part two

Tools for Radical
Self-Forgiveness

5 The Five Stages of Radical Self-Forgiveness

IN PART ONE, I BRIEFLY outlined the features and assumptions of Radical Self-Forgiveness and mentioned that the process itself comprises five stages. Every one of the tools that this technology provides guides us through these five stages. They are the same for both forgiving others and forgiving self. Let's now examine them in more detail.

STAGE 1: TELLING THE STORY

Whether we are a victim or a perpetrator of a wrongdoing, we will always have a story about what happened. All of the pain and suffering will be contained in the story, so having that story heard, witnessed, and validated is the first step in creating the space for forgiveness or self-forgiveness to occur. From this point on, for the sake of clarity, I will refer only to how this process works for self-forgiveness.

When telling the story, even if you are telling it to yourself by using one of the technologies contained herein, it is important not to overlay the victim/perpetrator story with any spiritual interpretations. You must pretend to know nothing at all about Radical Self-Forgiveness at this stage. Nor should you make excuses for yourself or attempt to explain the situation in ways that would tend to justify your actions. Don't even try to distinguish between appropriate and inappropriate guilt at this point. All of those things come in later stages.

It is during this stage that you give your judging self full reign to rant and rave against you for what it thinks you have done wrong. This is the judging self's great moment, so let your judging self have it. It needs to be heard and validated, loved and accepted, just like any other part of you. You will no doubt hear the voice of the critical parent, as well.

STAGE 2: FEELING THE FEELINGS

Every perpetrator story has a bundle of emotion attached to it. Yes, guilt and shame will be the primary feelings, but anger, fear, regret, remorse, and a whole host of other similar emotions will be right up there with the guilt and shame. Whatever they are, the important thing is to feel them fully. You cannot heal what you don't feel.

The definition of an emotion is "a thought attached to a feeling," but the bond between the thought and the feeling is very tight. You cannot break that bond simply by trying to change the thought alone, as in talk therapy or other similar modalities—the feeling component is the part that forms the bond, not the thought. Before the feeling can release the thought, and before an alternative thought can be emotionally accepted in its place, the feeling has to be reexperienced. It need not be experienced with the same intensity as originally felt, but it must at least be engaged in some way.

It helps to realize, too, that there is no such thing as a negative feeling. Feelings such as guilt, shame, fear, anger, sadness, or grief are not negative. They are simply normal human emotions we all feel from time to time to varying degrees. Labeling them as negative results in our struggling against them, trying to "think positive," or denying them. This only leads us to suppress, repress, and project them onto others, onto our own bodies, or onto situations. Resistance to any of our human emotions creates serious internal stress and ultimately causes disease.

Another way to resist feelings is to engage in constructing a *spiritual bypass*. Many people, especially those who think of themselves as spiritual, think that feelings are to be meditated away, rather than felt. It's important to acknowledge that many people in helping professions are also bypassers, addicted to helping others as a way of avoiding their own feelings and emotional pain.

Having been blessed with the capability to feel our emotions, it is natural that we should want the full experience of them. This means feeling them—not talking about them, analyzing them, or labeling them. When we do not allow ourselves to experience the full range of emotions but suppress them instead, our souls create situations in which we are *forced* to feel them. Have you noticed that people are often given opportunities to feel intense emotions just after having prayed for spiritual growth?

This idea suggests that the whole point of creating an upset may simply lie in our soul's desire to provide an opportunity for us to properly feel emotion. That being the case, simply allowing ourselves to have the feeling might let the energy move through us and cause the so-called problem to disappear immediately. This often happens. It's important to note that not all situations are dissolved so easily. When we have committed a crime regarded as unforgivable, such as sexual abuse, rape, theft, murder, and so on, it takes more than just experiencing our emotions to get to the point where we can truly forgive ourselves, radically or otherwise.

STAGE 3: COLLAPSING THE STORY

Completing this step represents the end of the line as far as traditional forgiveness is concerned. This is because traditional forgiveness makes its appeal to the human self, and so the process must end at this point—there's nowhere else to go.

It is in this third step that we ask the judging self to give way to the self-loving self. We need it to bring some heart-centered energy to the situation. It's the self-loving self's job at this stage to say to the judging self: "*Yes, but have some compassion for me and try to understand why I did what I did. Yes, I am a flawed human being, and I did something wrong, but if those who are judging me could imagine what it might have been like for them, had they been walking in my shoes at that time, under the same bad conditions and with all the emotional baggage I was carrying, they might not be so judgmental. So, Mr. Judging Self and all those others out there who are criticizing me, do cut me some slack here, please. If you cannot, at least try to imagine me as I once was when I was a tiny baby—innocent, unspoiled, whole, loving, and trusting of those around me, a beautiful child of God.* "

Opening our hearts to ourselves in this way, and asking others to do the same, helps us see ourselves as human beings with all our frailties and imperfections and allows us to become open to the possibility of being loved as we are. This is going to help us a great deal, too, in the Radical Self-Acceptance aspect, since this is what is meant by that phrase "loving ourselves exactly the way we are."

Bringing compassion and empathy to a situation that needs forgiveness also has the effect of reducing the intensity of the other feelings that we have experienced about our crime, such as anger, self-recrimination, shame, and so on. It won't do much about the guilt, though, since this process is directly related to what we did rather than how we interpreted it. However, this is also the step where we bring our rational minds to bear on the situation and ask ourselves some straightforward questions, like whether we are entitled to feel guilty. In other words, as we've already asked during this process, are our guilt and remorse appropriate or inappropriate?

If we find our guilt to be totally inappropriate, then there is nothing more we need to do. But even if we find that the guilt was appropriate, all we can do from a traditional-forgiveness standpoint is exercise our compassion and understanding, make a rational assessment of the situation, and then make the decision to forgive ourselves. But that's easier said than done, and unfortunately traditional forgiveness offers little that would help us make such a decision. On the other hand, Radical Self-Forgiveness provides a way that is simple, quick, and easy.

STAGE 4: REFRAMING THE STORY

This is the first unique step of Radical Self-Forgiveness and is the one that takes us beyond traditional forgiveness. That's because it asks us to let go of the idea that something wrong happened.

Remember, the prevailing worldview to which we all primarily subscribe is still one that is largely anchored in victim consciousness. This paradigm suggests that life is a game of chance and a matter of fighting for survival in a dog-eat-dog world. As we normally place our perpetrator story in this context, it seems self-evidently true. However, this fourth stage invites us to consider approaching our perpetrator story from a radically different angle.

We might illustrate this shift by referencing the paradigms listed in chapter 4 and picking out the ones that most accurately reflect the different contexts. For instance, we might say that paradigm 1 represents the prevailing worldview, while paradigm 5 represents the metaphysical worldview that would support a Radical Self-Forgiveness perspective. Let's see how this would work.

Paradigm 1

I take a rather scientific/secular/rational view of life. I think that human beings are simply part of the evolutionary spiral and that, like every other animal on the planet, we are born, we live, and then we die. Yes, there's a lot more to it, but that's more or less it in a nutshell. I am not a strong believer in a deity (God), though I wouldn't go so far as to call myself an atheist. I am not inclined to think there is a reality beyond what I register with my five senses. If there is, I have no real idea what that might be like. I am certainly not in touch with it and wouldn't know how to talk about it. Until now, forgiveness to me has meant making a conscious decision to let bygones be bygones.

Paradigm 5

I am a spiritual being having a human experience. By that I mean that I have chosen to come to Earth in order to learn lessons and evolve spiritually. This is the school, and life is the curriculum. What happens during my life are my lessons. I have come into the life experience with the desire to fully grasp what oneness is by experiencing the opposite of it—separation. I had made agreements with souls prior to my incarnation that they would do things not so much *to* me, though it will feel that way while I am in a body, but *for* me. I also enroll others while I'm here to give me opportunities to learn. They look like my enemies, but I see them as my healing angels. That's how I see forgiveness—that everything that happens invariably occurs for a spiritual purpose and that, while I remain accountable for what I do in the human world, in purely spiritual terms nothing wrong ever happens.

To adjust this paradigm to be applicable to self-forgiveness, we would only need to change the following sentences:

I had made agreements with souls prior to my incarnation that I would do things not so much to other people, though it will feel that way while I am in a body, but *for* them. While I'm here, others will enroll me to give them opportunities to learn. I will look like their enemy, but they will come to see me as their healing angel.

Altering the paradigm in this way shifts it from a victim story to a perpetrator story. It is necessary to make this explicit because, while we seem ready and willing to forgive others on the basis that they have come into our lives to do seemingly "bad" things to us (for us), so we can learn and grow, we seem to have difficulty accepting that we at times are called upon to play the role of perpetrator in order to be of service to others. We need to realize that for every victim, there must be a victimizer.

The reframe can be shown diagrammatically whereby we first show the story framed by all the thoughts, ideas, and beliefs contained in Paradigm 1. This represents our normal way of looking at how things happen. Then we show the story again, but this time framed by Paradigm 5. The story itself is not changed. (See figure 3.)

What has changed is the meaning and the context of the story, not the story itself. That puts an entirely different light on the apparent situation or event and enables us to move beyond merely letting bygones be bygones to opening to the possibility that nothing wrong happened and there is nothing to forgive.

Now, it's one thing to understand this intellectually; it is quite another to get it deep down in your body, especially if you have a really big perpetrator story to tell. For as long as you have had your perpetrator story, it has been alive in every cell of your body. The objective in this stage, then, is to

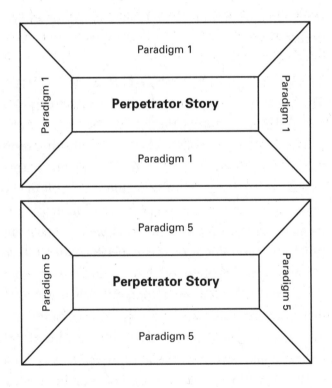

FIGURE 3   Perpetrator Story

replace the old story with the new (Radical Self-Forgiveness) story, so it gets fully anchored in your body in place of the old one.

To clearly illustrate a reframe that involves a perpetrator story, I have written a fictional story, which follows at the end of this chapter. I think by the time you have finished reading it, you will have begun to understand that there are no mistakes and no accidents.

STAGE 5: INTEGRATING THE SHIFT

The integration stage includes doing something of a physical nature during the Radical Self-Forgiveness process so that the body registers the transformation, as well as the mind. The original perpetrator story existed as an energy pattern within every cell of the body. This step involves replacing that old story and its associated energy pattern with the new interpretation that everything is or was in perfect order. I liken the integration process to what we do with our computer and the programs it contains. When we get a new program that supercedes one we already have installed, we uninstall the old one and then install the new one and save it to the hard drive. This is what we are doing with our stories, and our bodies are the equivalent of the hard drive. Our bodies are also the antennae for our Spiritual Intelligence, so doing something physical as part of the process ensures that our Spiritual Intelligence is activated. In some cases, the process involves doing breath work, in others it is walking across a circle, in others it is writing, and in all cases it is in using the voice. Some of these practices will be explored and used in upcoming chapters. But first, the following fiction story will demonstrate how a dramatic change in the context of what happened can shift one's perspective of the event in a profound way.

SUSAN'S STORY

Nothing focuses the mind more than the prospect of imminent death. Susan Phillips lay on her hard bed in the special cell she had been moved to the day before, close to where she was to die by lethal injection the next day. She was to be executed for the cold-blooded murder of her husband, Dan, thirteen years prior. A woman of slight build and medium height, with dark-brown hair and eyes to match, she was acting cool, but her insides were shaking. She was terrified.

Susan hadn't had a visit from anyone in the last five years. Susan's brother, Bob, had kept up his visits for a lot longer than anyone else, but even he had stopped coming. Both of their parents were dead, and he was her only relative. The last time he had visited her, it had been a tense and awkward meeting. Neither of them knew what to say. She was wallowing in shame and tried to cover it up by being hardnosed and aggressive, while he said very little.

Outwardly at least, it seemed that Susan's mother had taken it the worst. She was the first to go. She developed breast cancer and died at age sixty-five, soon after Susan was sentenced to death. She never got beyond the denial stage, always refusing to believe that her little Susan could kill someone, especially Dan, the son-in-law she adored. Susan's father died two years after his wife, not lasting but ten days after suffering a stroke at age sixty-nine.

Susan lay there thinking of her family and how she had effectively killed her parents and ruined her brother's life by her actions. She had lived with that guilt for the entire ten years she had been confined to her cell on death row.

But today, the feeling was more intense than ever and virtually palpable. It hung over her like a dark, ominous cloud and enveloped her whenever she closed her eyes, almost choking her. Tomorrow, she would pay with her life for all that she had done to hurt those she loved. In spite of the terror she was feeling for what she was soon to face, there was a part of her that felt good about paying the ultimate price for what she had done to hurt them. At least she would be free of the guilt and shame—maybe.

Susan was twenty-five when she met Dan. He was handsome, tall, and athletic, with a seemingly uncontrollable shock of blonde hair. His blue eyes sparkled with life, and he exuded a quiet and gentle confidence in how he handled himself in the company of others. Eventually Susan fell for him and married him when she was twenty-eight.

It was a seemingly ideal marriage, with both Susan and Dan bringing in a lot of income, which soon materialized outwardly as a big, expensive house in the best part of town. They started a family after three years of marriage. Susan gave birth to two boys, just two years apart, named Jay and Chris.

The marriage had become routine and dull. Dan was addicted to his work and spent little time at home. When he was there, he had little of any consequence to say to Susan, and she didn't offer much by way of compensation in order to keep the relationship lively.

She wasn't a bad attorney, but her heart wasn't in it. She didn't bring her work home like those who were more ambitious were prone to do. She did the minimum. She was bored with her work and her marriage.

Such circumstances made it possible for Susan to look outside her marriage for stimulation, which is how her relationship with Jerry came to fruition. Jerry was a computer technician. He came to the house to fix Susan's computer and to set up a network in her home office. This necessitated him being there for a couple of days, enough time for the chemistry they had both felt within moments of his first arrival to become physically expressed. They were in bed together on the second day.

Jerry was single, free, and a lot younger than Susan. With dark-brown hair cut very short and a pale complexion, he wasn't particularly good looking, but he had an energy that was irresistible to her. He was a free spirit and beholden to no one. Sexually, he was everything she had ever dreamed of but had never experienced with Dan.

What started out as a torrid sexual adventure turned into something much more intense. Jerry became obsessed with Susan, and in the coming weeks would not leave her alone. He was there at every opportunity. Susan very much enjoyed the attention and the sex but worried that they would be caught if they continued seeing each other so often, especially at her own house. She tried to put a stop to it, but neither she nor Jerry could bear not seeing each other. Theirs had turned into a powerful love affair and had a momentum all of its own.

Jerry pleaded with her to come away with him— to divorce Dan and marry him. To Susan it sounded like paradise, even if it meant losing her kids. She knew that Dan and his parents would take care of them, so the kids wouldn't suffer that much. But there was one big snag, and that was money.

Susan and Jerry had countless arguments about the money issue, and it was clearly the one sticking point. It was getting in the way of their blissful happiness— that was how she saw it. Poverty and happiness didn't go together in her mind. Even if she divorced Dan and got half of the assets, the house was mortgaged to the hilt, so she wouldn't come out with very much, certainly not enough to sustain her in her relatively extravagant lifestyle.

Slowly an idea formed in her mind. There was a way out. Dan had a life insurance policy that was worth five million dollars. If he were to die, she would inherit the five million and the rest of the estate. *Now, that would make it work,* she thought. She caught herself thinking this way and it scared her. She tried to put the idea out of her mind, but every time it reentered she would find a way to justify it. In time, it began to seem like the right thing to do. Once that decision was made, the only question left was: how could she make it happen?

It was a measure of how irrational the whole affair had made her that she could even think this way. Even more so, that she made herself believe that she could get away with it. But this is exactly how she now thought about it, putting out of her mind that it was an immoral thing to do. To her, at that time, it was simply a matter of being pragmatic. It would solve her problem, and she would be with her beloved Jerry. The two boys would go with Dan's parents. *They would do a much better job of raising them anyway,* she thought. Susan never did think of herself as much of a mother.

Susan did not talk to Jerry about her plan. He would have opposed it immediately, of course. She scoured the Internet, looking for information on poisons that would leave no trace and that would sufficiently mimic some condition known to medical science to satisfy a coroner as to the cause of death. Acting according to one set of instructions Susan found, she put the poison in Dan's food slowly over a period of two weeks. As it began to take effect, Dan became progressively sicker, and even as a doctor, he couldn't understand why. But having a big professional ego, he didn't want to consult another doctor, so he treated himself for what he thought it might be. He was, of course, mistaken. He died within three weeks of Susan administering the first dose.

Though heart failure was officially given as the cause of death, the police were suspicious and began an investigation. The insurance company also insisted on an inquiry into the sudden death of an otherwise healthy man with a policy worth five million dollars. Suspecting poisoning, the police confiscated all the kitchen utensils and the food in Susan's cupboards and refrigerator, but they didn't find anything. Susan did have the good sense to make sure that she had sterilized everything that had contained the poison, and had disposed of anything that might have had a trace of the terrible stuff. She had also done her homework well on the

Internet because as promised, the poison did not show up in Dan's body during the autopsy. Heart failure seemed to be the legitimate cause of death.

But by now the media had gotten hold of the story, and they began the usual "trial by media." Susan was described as "a person of interest" by the police, and the media kept up the heat. It was a reporter who discovered Susan's liaison with Jerry, which, combined with a five million dollar payout on the victim's life, added a lot more juice to the story. The suspicion that Susan had killed Dan for his money became so intense that Jerry demanded that Susan tell him what was going on.

"I did it for us," Susan admitted.

"What did you do?" screamed Jerry.

"Dan wasn't happy, and we are. Now we can be together forever."

"What are you talking about?" demanded Jerry.

"It was the only way," replied Susan softly.

"You killed him? Are you out of your mind?"

"It's OK. They won't know. It will blow over. There's no proof. The press will go away soon. I love you, Jerry."

"This is crazy!" Jerry spat. "I gotta get out of here!"

"No! Please don't go. It's gonna be OK. Don't leave me alone, Jerry. We have to be together."

Jerry was now clearly in a panic and way beyond being persuaded. All he could see was the possibility of his precious freedom being taken away from him, and he could not bear to contemplate that. Even though he was in an agitated state of mind, it was clear to him that he could be implicated for the murder, and he wanted no part of it. He loved Susan, but not enough to become embroiled in a murder case and be charged as an accessory. He left hurriedly, making it crystal clear that he was never going to be coming back.

Susan was devastated, but she made up her mind that if she was caught and convicted she would make sure that Jerry didn't stay free for long. She would tell the authorities that he was part of it, knew about the plan all along, and had supported it.

Susan had covered her tracks well as far as the act of poisoning was concerned, but she hadn't thought about what might still be on her hard drive as a result of all her research. When the forensic experts examined the hard drive, they found everything that she had ever downloaded from the Internet and were able to retrieve it. They soon had the evidence they needed to charge her with first-degree murder.

When her case came to court, Susan tried to implicate Jerry right from the beginning by entering a plea of guilty by reason of insanity, saying that he had poisoned her mind and brainwashed her into killing Dan so he could have the money. The jury didn't buy it, but they did buy her false testimony that Jerry knew about it and encouraged her. He got fifteen years, and she got her revenge.

As she lay there, Susan was wishing she believed in God. She was absolutely terrified and was becoming more so by the minute. She would have loved to have had something to hang on to and pray to. She had never felt more alone and scared in her life. One more dreadful night to endure, probably sleepless, and then—the unthinkable.

Mercifully, in spite of everything that she was feeling, sleep was beginning to overtake her. Her eyes were becoming heavy, and her breathing was slowing and becoming more rhythmic.

Suddenly, she became aware of a light emanating from somewhere above her, illuminating the cramped cell. The light got brighter and very soon became intense. Susan didn't know whether she was asleep or not, or whether she was imagining it. Even though her eyes remained closed, she did a reality check and realized that she was still lying on her bed in her cell, and that tomorrow she was going to die. This was no alternate reality—it was the same reality she had been living for ten years.

But the light was something else altogether—like nothing she had ever experienced before. Even more extraordinary was that all her fear and terror had completely disappeared. All she could feel was a profound sense of peace enveloping her entire body like a down quilt.

A few moments passed, and then, even though her eyes were still closed, she became aware of a form gradually taking shape within the light. It vaguely resembled a human, but the light being so bright, Susan could make out no features or edges. But what she could feel was a deep and overwhelming sense of unconditional love emanating from this being. When it spoke to her, it was as if the voice was in her head, and yet it seemed entirely real.

"Hello, Susan." The voice was smooth and soft.

"Who are you? What are you?" whispered Susan. "Am I just dreaming this or are you real?"

"I've come to you in your dream state, but I am real enough," replied the being. "I'm here to help you make your journey to the other side and to ease the way for you. Had I come while you were in your full waking state, fear would have prevented you from being aware of my presence. While we angels do our work unseen most of the time, in your case we wanted to become manifest."

"We? There's only one of you," said Susan.

"I appear as one individual to you right now, but in truth we are a collective. In this form I am representing many souls and many angels, especially the ones who have been working with you."

"Why are you here?" asked Susan.

"We see the guilt and pain that you are in and we wish to alleviate those feelings as you prepare to make your transition to the other side," the being explained.

"Do you do this with everyone?" asked Susan.

"Yes, to a greater or lesser degree. But, as I said we most often do it in a way that precludes any awareness. Some people think of it as a premonition of their impending death, but for the most part, people don't even know."

"Then why have you made yourself known to me?" asked Susan. "I'm not religious and have never believed in God. Even now as I face my death, I still don't believe."

"It's not necessary in the least," replied the being reassuringly. "Everyone is cared for just the same. We make no distinctions. Your beliefs are irrelevant."

"But there are others in this prison more worthy than I am to be given this chance," pleaded Susan. "Many of them are not actually guilty of the crimes for which they have been convicted, but I really am guilty—I killed my husband in cold blood. I deserve to feel guilty, and I deserve to die. I am not in the least bit worthy to receive your help."

"Apparently, someone on this side disagrees with you," replied the being. "Someone you know well."

"Who?"

"Susan, it's me—Dan."

Susan was now in complete shock. She still wasn't sure whether this was all a dream and couldn't make out whether that voice, which certainly sounded like Dan's, was in her head or coming from near the being. Perhaps both.

"I know this must be a shock, Susan," Dan's voice continued. "I insisted on it, though, so it's my fault. I couldn't bear to see you in such terrible pain. Usually this doesn't happen until after you die, but I wanted you to have the knowledge going into tomorrow, given the state you'll be in."

The being spoke, "Before you incarnated, Susan, I was your Angel of Incarnation, which means that I was the one that who helped you plan your life. My name is Harley. You and I, along with your soul group, which included Dan, Jerry, your mother and father, and a number of others, planned it down to the smallest detail. And I have to say it has worked out pretty well so far."

"Wait a minute," interrupted Susan, "What do you mean we planned it all? That's crazy! Why would I plan this horrible outcome?"

"It's true, Susan," Dan interjected. "I wouldn't have believed it either when I was on that side. As you know, I was closed to anything other than scientific reality. But as soon as I passed over and got acclimated to the new vibration, I began to realize that my view of life on Earth, while it was true in terms of earthbound reality, was not the real truth. It was all an illusion. The truth lay elsewhere.

"I soon came to see that we, as intelligent spiritual beings, deliberately choose to incarnate into human form, sometimes many times over, in order to learn lessons that will help us to evolve spiritually. The idea that we are 'fallen' and that God is mad at us is not true at all. And believe me, there is no hell."

"Prison is my version of hell," rejoined Susan.

"I can understand that," replied Dan, who after a pause continued, "It wasn't long before I was reunited with those in my soul group who had remained or had incarnated and come back home before me. I was taken through my life review and saw how everything that had ever happened to me was all part of my plan for the particular incarnation that had just ended."

"Including being murdered by me?" quipped Susan, who was rightfully skeptical.

"Yes, including being murdered by you," replied Dan without missing a beat. "We agreed upon it in advance of our incarnation. It was all part of our soul contract."

"And what about Jerry? Was he in on the plot, too?" Susan asked. "If it hadn't been for him, I wouldn't have killed you, Dan. There was no other reason to."

"Of course, he was," interjected Harley. "Jerry played a very crucial role in this whole drama. He had his own lessons to learn, too, of course, just as we all do when we go down to the earth plane. He is fulfilling his soul journey by being incarcerated for fifteen years."

"Are you saying he chose that?" demanded Susan incredulously. "He chose fifteen years in prison just to learn a lesson?"

"He needed you to trigger his intense fear of loss of freedom by first involving him in the murder, and then just when he thought he had ensured his freedom by bolting from the relationship, you turned around and betrayed him. That enabled him to do the prison time he needed to do."

"Now, let's get this straight," said Susan. "Are you also saying that I actually chose to murder my husband, live in this rathole for ten years or more, and end up being executed as a murderer? I chose this in order to learn some kind of lesson?"

"It's true, honey," said a new voice that Susan recognized as her mother. "It's exactly as Harley says. Dad and I have been here with Dan ever since we both died."

"You, too!" cried Susan. "Don't tell me you're part of this, as well!"

"We were," answered her father's voice. "We were all in this together. And we've done it many times before, too."

"Oh, and what was I supposed to get out of murdering Dan and spending the rest of my life in prison?" Susan responded. "What lesson was I supposed to learn?"

"Susan, you are not ready to have that revealed to you yet," said Harley lovingly. "That will become clear when you get to the other side and complete your life review. You and I will meet again to go through that process. Everything will be revealed then."

"What's the point of all this then?" asked Susan. "Dan, Mom, Dad, why have you all come here on this day, of all days?"

"We came to let you know that in reality you did not make a mistake," her father explained. "When you look at it from this side, it becomes clear that neither you nor anyone else has ever done anything wrong."

"Are you telling me that I am not really guilty of murder?" asked Susan.

"Susan, it is not that you are not guilty in human terms," Harley explained. "Of course, you are. You killed your husband, so you are guilty of the crime of murder. Whatever happens in the World of Humanity is governed by human law, at least on the surface. So the fact is that you committed a murder, and you are paying the price.

In the spirit world, you can't actually kill anyone. As souls, we are immortal. When we die, we simply shift to a different vibration and continue to exist on a different plane. So on one level, you killed Dan, but on another level, you didn't. You just enabled him to release his body at the time previously agreed upon."

"But what about the children?" Susan replied. "Why do they have to suffer because of what I did?"

"Their souls chose it, too, Susan," Dan interjected. "They are part of our soul group, as well.

In fact, they are both very old souls with a great deal of wisdom, so their input during the planning sessions was invaluable. They have chosen to experience a lot in this lifetime around compassion and forgiveness. In fact, their first real test begins tomorrow when they watch you die."

"They hate me, though," said Susan sadly.

"Yes, and they will continue to do so for a long while," Harley responded.

Susan began to feel an overwhelming sense of guilt for having devastated her kids' lives. Harley picked up on her thoughts and feelings immediately. "Don't go there, Susan," he said. "No need for any more guilt. The kids are doing their journey just fine, according to their own plans. You've experienced all the guilt you needed to, so now is the time to acknowledge and appreciate your soul's willingness to take on such a difficult lesson."

Susan felt tears streaming down her cheeks. She hadn't cried for years, but lots of wonderful emotions were welling up inside her. She was overcome by a feeling of deep love for herself and a sense of profound self-acceptance for all that she was and had been as a human being. All the guilt and pain drained away. Even the execution seemed less daunting. She would go through it with grace and humility.

Suddenly, the light was no more, and for the first time since she had fallen asleep, she opened her eyes. Nothing. Just the cell walls and her few belongings. Had it all been just a dream? Had she imagined it all, simply as a way to psychologically prepare for the execution?

It didn't take very long for her to realize that no dream or trick of the mind could have transformed her consciousness to this degree. The feelings of self-love and self-acceptance she was experiencing were beyond anything she had ever known, and she recognized it as pure grace. She knew she had experienced true forgiveness—Radical Forgiveness.

Susan awoke the next morning, roused by the guards. They couldn't help but notice that something was different about her. She seemed strangely altered in some way. She seemed at peace. The only explanation they had was that perhaps she had found God at the last minute.

The execution was scheduled for 6:00 p.m. Shortly before that time, four people from Dan's family were led into their viewing room. They included Dan's brother and two sisters and one of their spouses. On the other side of the wall, in their own room, sat Susan's children Chris and Jay, and her brother, Bob. Although separated by a wall, the two groups could see the window and had a clear view of what was happening on the other side.

Susan was already there, strapped to a gurney. The chaplain was there with her and would remain throughout the procedure.

"Finally," said one of the sisters, "we get to see justice done. I'm glad I'm here to see her die. I've been waiting a long time for this."

Susan looked out through the window at those gathered, first at her sons and her brother. She looked the two boys fully in the eyes, and through the glass, mouthed, "I love you." She simply smiled the smile of a mother. There was no agenda attached to it—just love. She smiled at Bob and mouthed the same thing.

As the first round of drugs was administered, Susan's eyes closed for the last time. The rooms were silent. No one spoke. No one moved. The execution took approximately eight minutes.

Once she was pronounced dead, both families were led out and escorted to their respective prear-ranged press conferences. Microphones and cameras were set up, and reporters were seated at tables. As usual, eager reporters asked the victim's family members how they were feeling now that justice had been served and a dangerous killer had been removed from decent society. *Were they able to get closure now and feel able to get on with their lives?*, the reporters demanded.

Strangely enough, as much as the reporters tried to get them to talk like victims and paint Susan as the villain, the family seemed not to want to take the bait. In fact, they found themselves strangely reticent to talk at all, even though Dan's sisters had intended to release a whole load of venom about Susan at the earliest opportunity. To their own consternation, they seemed unable to find the words to express the feelings they did have—primarily because they themselves didn't know exactly what they were feeling.

In fact, they had seen something in Susan's eyes. As she looked out through that window, just before she closed her eyes for the last time, it seemed as though she was communicating something. Everyone had felt it, no one knew what it was, and not one person mentioned it.

After the press conferences, they went through their debriefings, and then everyone went their separate ways, back to their day-to-day lives. But there was not one of them who did not feel that they had been forever changed by the experience. And not one of them knew why.

I would not be at all surprised if you are in shock after reading this story. After all, it is the kind of story that would make some of what you see on *Dateline* seem quite tame. And had they run it, they would certainly have painted Susan as heartless, wicked, and most likely beyond redemption. However, I confess that I wrote this story with the full intention to make Susan's crime extreme in order to make the point that no matter how bad the crime seems, the principle holds that, at the spiritual level, there was no crime committed.

What needs to be understood is that with Radical Forgiveness and Radical Self-Forgiveness there can be no exceptions. They either apply to everything or nothing. There are no half measures. The extent to which you want to make a distinction according to how serious the crime was indicates how little you understand the underlying principles of this form of forgiveness—self or otherwise. If you cannot identify with Susan and see that, at the spiritual level, she did exactly what needed to be done for everyone involved, then you don't yet understand Radical Forgiveness.

According to the Radical Self-Forgiveness philosophy, even though Susan, as a human being, was guilty of a terrible murder, at the spiritual level she was no more a perpetrator of a crime than her murdered husband was a victim of one. The point of this story is to illustrate the difference and to drive home the true nature of the reframe.

It is designed to prevent people from avoiding a truly spiritual interpretation of what happened by simply sugarcoating the situation. "Such and such happened, but I got this from it,"—that is not a reframe.

As the story is written, there is no way to sugarcoat what Susan did in human terms. Nothing less than a full spiritual reframe as described in this book could make some sense of this situation and represent the key to real self-forgiveness.

In the next chapter, I describe a potent Radical Self-Forgiveness practice that Susan might have used to forgive herself had Harley not appeared. It will help us to see how we might forgive ourselves in the same way. It is called the Three Letters Process.

6 The Three Letters Process

THE THREE LETTERS PROCESS IS a powerful way to help people go through the five stages of Radical Forgiveness. The idea is simple, but I will explain it first as if you were writing the letters from the point of view of a victim. I will then tell you how to apply the same process to Radical Self-Forgiveness. After outlining what goes in each letter, I will demonstrate how to construct the three self-forgiveness letters by writing them as if it were Susan, our fictional character from chapter 5, writing them. I suggest that you wait one day between writing each letter, but not more than forty-eight hours. Please note: If you are writing the letters from a victim's standpoint, you must never send any of the three letters to the person you are forgiving. I recommend destroying them after having written the third one.

WRITING THE LETTERS FROM
A VICTIM'S STANDPOINT

From the perspective of the one who is injured, write your first letter to the perpetrator, telling him, her, or it (it might be a nonhuman entity like an institution, government, church, or group) how much you have suffered and been damaged by what they have done, or are doing, to you. Say exactly how you are feeling and hold back nothing. This is the equivalent of the first two stages of this process—telling the story and feeling the feelings.

The next day, write another letter to the same person or entity, but this time write it from more of a heart space. Do your best to have some compassion for them and some understanding of why they did what they did or are still doing to you. It's important to recognize that you are not letting them off the hook, because even though you are willing to cut them some slack, you are still saying they did, or are doing, something detrimental. This is the equivalent of stage three—collapsing the story. As we've discussed, the first three stages of this process are equivalent to traditional forgiveness, so this second letter is as far as you could go under that system.

But with Radical Forgiveness, you have the luxury of being able to write an additional letter in which you acknowledge that you have come to see the whole situation from a different perspective, which has helped to illuminate the fact that what happened was divinely planned. You now see that it had to happen this way for a reason, one that has everything to do with your spiritual growth. You also recognize the likelihood that you enrolled this person to come into your life to perform these acts, not *to* you but *for* you.

That means that nothing wrong ever really happened and that there is nothing to forgive. This third letter is equivalent to the fourth stage of the Radical Forgiveness process—reframing the story. This letter will often transform the situation immediately, because it will be interpreted by your Spiritual Intelligence as a secular prayer, and as such, it will be acted upon.

Bear in mind that all forgiveness is a "fake-it-till-you-make-it" proposition, so it is very likely that you will have to fake some of what you choose to include in letter #2. You will almost certainly have to fake what goes in letter #3. It doesn't matter, though—just writing this third letter shows the right intention, and that is all your Spiritual Intelligence needs to register for your letter to become a secular prayer.

WRITING THE LETTERS FROM
A PERPETRATOR'S STANDPOINT

As the self-confessed perpetrator of some injury against another person or entity, you must write the first letter to yourself, lambasting yourself for what you have done. Guess whose services you will solicit to help you write this letter? Of course, your judging self. Your judging self will relish the task and will launch a tirade of criticism against you, trying hard to make you feel as guilty as possible. It will feel as if you are channeling your judging self when writing this letter.

In the second letter, begin to retire the judging self to some degree and start channeling your inner lover. This alternate opinion will provide some counterpoint to your judging self's strident criticism by bringing some compassion and understanding to your situation, sufficient at least to reduce the level of guilt and shame within you and for you to feel accepted.

In the third letter, which is the reframe, you write to your I Am Self. In this letter, you recognize that what you did was meant to happen for whatever reason and declare your understanding that there is nothing for which you need to be forgiven at the spiritual level.

Susan's Three Perpetrator Letters

Letter #1

Susan,

You are a stupid little fool! What a crazy thing to do! And for such selfish reasons, too. If you wanted Jerry that badly, why didn't you just go with him and take a chance on life? Oh no, that wouldn't do, would it? You had to have money, too, to support your selfish spendthrift ways, didn't you? And you were prepared to kill for them, weren't you? Your own husband no less. How low can you get? You are nothing but scum.

How could you be so coldhearted and cruel to even think of killing your wonderful husband? What did he ever do to you that he might deserve that? Nothing. Day after day, you sat there at your computer searching for information to help you kill him. That's cold-blooded murder, Susan. You can't even say that it was a crime of passion. What a selfish, horrible, heartless bitch you are. Execution is too good for you. They ought to give you what you gave Dan, so you can take three weeks to die in pain and agony like he did. I hate you so much, I'd do it myself if I could. I'd watch you writhe in pain and agony and take great pleasure in offering you no help at all. You deserve no mercy whatsoever.

You were unfaithful to Dan from the start. And when Jerry came along, you wasted no time at all jumping into bed with him, did you? What did you care? It's all about Susan, isn't it? To hell with the others in your life.

And how much did you think about those two boys? Hardly at all, right? Never mind that you were prepared to take their father away from them forever by killing the poor guy, and willing to see them traumatized by the whole thing, but you were ready to pawn them off on Dan's parents just so you could go away with Jerry and be alone. What kind of a mother are you? No wonder they hate you. How could it be otherwise? You are so loathsome, Susan. And look at how what you did affected your mother and father. It killed them both in the end, and for sure it broke their hearts. After all they did for you. They were great parents. They loved you and gave you a good start in life, and look what you did with it. Killed your husband and ended up on death row. What a waste of a life. How stupid to think you could get away with it.

Letter #2
Dearest Susan,
Oh, what a deluded, lovesick idiot you were to even imagine that killing your husband was the answer

to your problem. I can only imagine that you were, in some way, out of your mind—delusional, in fact.

No rational, sane person would have done what you did. And yet, a part of me is able to understand it, because I know from my own experience that when love hits you very hard, it has a force of its own. It can take you over completely and make you do things that you would ordinarily never think of doing. It's as though you are possessed by something that is not you. I'm sure that was how it was for you, right Susan?

I understand you were bored with your marriage and your job. That made you extremely vulnerable to being love-struck by someone like Jerry who was sexually exciting and interesting in so many different ways. He was everything you had been craving in your life, wasn't he? He offered you freedom, excitement, travel, great sex, and more. Once he had your heart, how could you resist? You had no choice but to find a way to escape from your current life, so you could run off with him. And in your mind you justified it. To you, it did seem like the only rational choice, didn't it?

And, Susan, I know that you would never have gotten used to poverty and insecurity. Even though you were besotted with him, you knew that Jerry potentially offered a lot of both, so I can see that it was a huge problem for you.

You've always liked expensive clothes and enjoyed a relatively lavish lifestyle, so I can sympathize with you in that regard. You have to learn to be poor, Susan, and I couldn't see you doing it. Money was very meaningful to you in every way, so I don't see it simply as greed like the media do. For you, it simply was a necessary ingredient in the whole plan, no question about it. But to kill your own husband for it, Susan? And without regard to your children's feelings and those of your parents and Dan's family?

Five million dollars must have been tempting, heaven knows; but no, I must come back to my original opinion that you could never have done these things had you not been out of your mind. I know you tried an insanity plea in court, but you only did that to try to finger Jerry. I think you should have pushed it for real and made it a strong and authentic plea on your own behalf. Your attorney could have argued a strong case for it, in my opinion, but they saw through your need for revenge and didn't buy it.

The reason I say you should have pled insanity is because I know that you are not a bad person and could not have done it in such a cruel way if you had been yourself. You are not a killer, Susan, especially not a cold-blooded, calculating, and cruel killer. I didn't think it then and still don't. I think the affair was so tumultuous, it put you over the edge into insanity, albeit for only a few weeks.

Love, like you had with Jerry, was enough to make anyone insane. In fact, it was the epitome of madness. How else can you explain how you, a warm, friendly person who had never done anything of that nature before in her entire life, could have murdered your husband in such a calculating way? And it's not as if he were unkind or cruel to you—just boring.

But when all is said and done, Susan, you did murder your husband. That is a fact. And you should be punished for it. But I want you to know that I still love you and accept you just the way you are, Susan. I know that you are neither any less nor any more of a flawed human being than any of the rest of us out here. You have made some bad mistakes in your life, and you are paying a heavy price for them, but who am I to say I wouldn't have done the same thing had I been walking in your shoes? What politician can, in all humility, claim that he or she has the moral right to say that a state-sanctioned murder of you is any better than your murder of Dan?

Farewell, dear Susan.

Letter #3

Dear Susan,

I write this now from the perspective of your I Am Self, with the knowledge and comfort that everything that has happened in your life, Susan, has run exactly according to plan and that everyone else in your life, who was seemingly affected by your actions, was in fact getting exactly what they were supposed to from all the situations, just as you were. It was all perfect.

Your ego and your judging self did a wonderful job in creating just the right amount of drama to enable you to experience the degree of pain of separation for which your soul enrolled. I must say, you left it a bit late, but you made up for it by choosing ten years of isolation on death row. It doesn't get more painful than that, does it? Add in the heartache of being separated from the love of your life, and you've achieved a significant amount of spiritual growth, my dear Susan. You were so brave and courageous to even consider enduring that much pain.

You had the benefit of having the whole plot revealed to you just before your death, as many people do, of course. You learned that your murder of Dan was a soul agreement made with him before you were born. He agreed to come into this life just for that purpose—to be murdered by you. That gave a lot of other people, like his own family, an opportunity to feel their own pain of separation, while providing you with the opening to create the jail experience.

Jerry, on the other hand, came for his own reasons, chief among them being to experience the pain of losing his precious freedom, as well as to help you. As part of your soul contract, it seems, he had agreed to abandon you, and you agreed to take his freedom away.

Judas and Jesus had a similar agreement. Without Judas, Jesus could not have gone on to give the great lesson he was destined to give, could he? Judas was perhaps the only soul willing to cause the death of the most beloved person ever to walk the face of the earth. It takes a great deal of love to play the role of a villain, Susan, and you did it really well.

It should now be clear to you that everything was, and still is, in divine order and that no mistakes were ever made. Your life has unfolded in a perfect manner, and everything that you did, however you behaved, and no matter what kind of person you became, it was exactly as it should have been. Nothing wrong ever happened, and there was never anyone, or anything, to forgive.

God bless you, dearest Susan.

As I indicated earlier, Radical Forgiveness is a "fake-it-till-you-make-it" process, and it is no less so with Radical Self-Forgiveness. In both cases, the first letter is easy to write because that will most likely reflect your state of mind at the time. Writing the second letter, though, is understandably much harder to do. You have to try really hard to find true compassion and understanding for the perpetrator or for yourself. And as already discussed, it seems to be the most difficult when we are trying to forgive ourselves. You may well have to fake quite a lot of the second letter.

But when it comes to writing the third letter, unless you have integrated into your everyday consciousness a way of thinking based on paradigm 6, described on page 119, you will almost certainly have to fake it. Remember, in Susan's case, she had the big advantage of being given the chance to see beyond the veil and to recognize the truth firsthand. Most of us don't have that luxury, so we have no choice but to put our skepticism to one side and fake the third letter.

But it makes no difference. Over the years, I and my team have proven beyond a shadow of a doubt that even though people write things in their third letter they don't really believe at the mental and emotional levels, their Spiritual Intelligence knows that it is the truth. Consequently, it allows the energy tied up in the illusion to automatically dissolve. They feel better immediately, no matter whether the guilt was appropriate or not.

Read Susan's letters several times over and use them as models of how to write these three letters for yourself whenever you are experiencing a lot of guilt or shame. The Three Letters Process is a powerful and potent tool for self-forgiveness and as a way to forgive others, so don't underestimate it. Try it for yourself and discover just how healing it can be.

7 Spiritual Intelligence

As a prelude to going deeper into the conceptual framework of Radical Self-Forgiveness and its methodology, you must first understand which part of our psyche is most involved in making it work. I've made brief references to Spiritual Intelligence throughout the book thus far, but I would like to explain it more thoroughly now.

THE THREE TYPES OF INTELLIGENCE

There are three types of intelligence that enable us to function in the world: mental intelligence, emotional intelligence, and Spiritual Intelligence. Let's examine each in turn.

We are all familiar with mental intelligence and the fact that it can be accurately measured through tests of many kinds. Mental intelligence is a highly developed faculty. Such intelligence is essentially responsible for all cognitive activity of the rational mind—thoughts, ideas, concepts, paradigms, theories, and so on. Among the many millions of things it has enabled us to do, mental intelligence has facilitated our visits to space, amazing medical procedures to cure disease, and our ability to develop sophisticated models of the world through science and mathematics. We might say that this form of intelligence defines the "intellectual human self."

Emotional intelligence, on the other hand, defines the "feeling human self." Whereas mental intelligence is located in the brain, emotional intelligence springs from the heart. Our emotional intelligence guides our emotional responses to life—whether fear driven, love driven, guilt driven, pleasure driven, and so on. It tells us when we are in denial, lying, or out of integrity. It enables our ability to relate to each other at the heart level with compassion, empathy, tolerance, humility, and forgiveness. Without emotional intelligence, we would either be stifled by our thoughts and unable to truly feel or be complete sociopaths unable to control our emotions.

EMOTIONS RULE
Because people are taught to value mental intelligence more and to deny their feelings, emotional intelligence is quite underdeveloped in humans.

However, it seems that our lives are driven far more by unconscious emotional responses than by rational thought. Allowing the power of our raw, unchecked emotions to override our mental intelligence often results in mental/emotional structures like bigotry, prejudice, unreasonable attitudes, inflexibility of mind, false beliefs, denial, and so on ruling our lives. We often believe what we want to believe, not what makes sense.

THE INTELLIGENCE OF THE I AM SELF

Whereas the energy driving mental and emotional intelligence emanates from the ego and is relatively coarse in nature, Spiritual Intelligence emanates from our I Am Self and is much finer and infinitely more subtle than the other two. Also, unlike the other two, it operates below the level of our awareness. It knows the truth of who we are and connects us to the World of Spirit and Universal Intelligence (God). Our bodies are the antennae for our Spiritual Intelligence.

Spiritual Intelligence guides us on our spiritual journey, always moving us in the direction of growth and healing. It is our internal spiritual compass and keeps us on track with our divine plan. It finds its outer expression in our everyday lives in the form of religious or spiritual practice, the search for meaning beyond this reality, contemplation and meditation, prayer, and so on. It is not bound by time and space.

When we ask for help from our I Am Self, that's when our Spiritual Intelligence comes to the fore. Of the three forms of intelligence, it is the only one that can connect directly with the I Am Self and the Divine. Since the tools and processes of Radical Forgiveness are designed to activate our Spiritual Intelligence, they provide a perfect way to ask for such divine assistance, even if we are genuinely skeptical about the whole idea. Without Spiritual Intelligence, "real" forgiveness—of self or otherwise—would not be achieved.

SECULAR PRAYER

When I first created the Radical Forgiveness Worksheet, I did not realize that it was in fact a form of what I now call "secular prayer." I didn't know that its purpose was to communicate with our Spiritual Intelligence and, furthermore, that it, and all the other tools that followed, actually moved spiritual energy and worked immediately to change peoples' lives. I soon discovered, however, that not only did it alter the lives of the people using it, it had a positive impact on much of what was causing the problems in the first place, often in ways that were simply amazing.

At first blush, the term *secular prayer* seems to be an oxymoron, since the Radical Forgiveness technology does not require you to have a belief in God. This would seem to preclude it from being a form of prayer, since to whom does one pray if not to God? However, to say that a belief in God is not necessary doesn't mean that you need not have a belief in some kind of power greater than yourself, which will likely become active in your life at the spiritual level when necessary. That much, at least, is required—even if you conceive of that power as being nothing more than your own Higher Self.

There is no requirement, however, that we know what that power is or how it operates. And we are certainly not obligated to accept anyone else's view on such topics. Since there's no definition that must be attached to it other than one's own personal ideas, Spiritual Intelligence can legitimately be thought of as a secular/metaphysical notion, assuming one chooses to see it that way. And yet, while the notion of secular prayer distinguishes Spiritual Intelligence from any particular religious or spiritual belief system, it is also true that people who employ a specific belief system find it easy to fit the Radical Forgiveness system into their existing beliefs. The process is extremely flexible in this regard, and allows us to simply use whatever notion of a Higher Power resonates most appropriately.

BE OPEN, YET SKEPTICAL

Another interesting thing I discovered was that the only thing required of a person doing the Radical Self-Forgiveness work is a willingness to be open to the possibility that, no matter how he or she thinks of it, Spiritual Intelligence can be accessed and used for good in his or her life simply by soliciting its guidance using the tools of Radical Forgiveness. When we make such requests, it is still a form of prayer, albeit of a more secular nature. Some sort of Higher Power is being invoked, even if we have no particular religious belief or a developed concept of what that Higher Power might be. And the effects of secular prayer can be the same as prayers to one's God—the only difference being in the manner of our asking. From a practical standpoint, since we see dramatic results when we use the Radical Self-Forgiveness tools, we can say that Radical Forgiveness connects us to the Divine in much the same way as traditional prayer, probably because both employ the services of our Spiritual Intelligence.

NO SPIRITUAL AMNESIA

No matter how we choose to conceive of the process by which we connect to the Divine, employing the term *Spiritual Intelligence* gives us a way to think about how the connection is maintained and how communication with our Higher Power is facilitated during our life as a human being. When we agreed to incarnate and subscribe to particular life lessons in order to further our souls' evolution, we fully understood the need to forget about the spirit world from which we had come and to have what I call "spiritual amnesia." Without such amnesia, it would be impossible for us to participate in the game of life as intended.

However, Spiritual Intelligence is a part of our psyche that is not subject to spiritual amnesia. It has always known the truth of who we are and remembers the divine plan for our lives. It also remains in direct communication with Universal Intelligence, a name I personally like to give to that Higher Power we were previously discussing.

THE EGO AS OUR GUIDE

Our Spiritual Intelligence works with the ego to create the circumstances of our lives, whether those that were decided prior to incarnation or those that were adopted opportunistically along the way. Our ego works with our Spiritual Intelligence to convince us that life, as we understand it, is real and that living in the world means trying to control as many aspects of it as possible. To this end, the ego tells us to strive to earn as much money as possible in order to become successful and accumulate as much material wealth as we can.

Ego tells us that the world is a dangerous place, that we can't really trust anyone else, and that it's a dog-eat-dog world. It tells us that life is a game of chance, has no real meaning, and is chaotic. We're essentially encouraged to live our lives from this shaky place and to continuously operate out of fear. Such a perspective is entirely purposeful, in the spiritual sense, in that it helps provide opportunities for us to experience the pain of separation. This is the basic lesson all human selves are here to learn—the nature of oneness.

Marshall McLuhan once famously said, "The last one to discover water is likely to be the fish." By that he meant that many who are totally immersed in a particular environment are completely unaware of it, which means that the only way to appreciate an experience is to be exposed to the opposite of it. For example, you cannot appreciate what darkness is until you have experienced light.

THE PURPOSE OF THE SOUL'S JOURNEY

So, in order to fully appreciate being in a state of oneness with Universal Intelligence, we must come into the human experience and this world of duality in order to know the opposite of oneness—separation. To truly experience this separation, not just as an idea but as an emotion—the definition of which is a thought attached to a feeling—we need a body. Without a body we would have no way of experiencing the emotional pain of separation, which is the whole purpose of the operation. Once we've experienced the necessary amount of separation, our Spiritual Intelligence allows us to begin awakening to the truth that this is our soul's journey and that everything we have been experiencing has a particular purpose.

The goal of the ego, then, working through our Spiritual Intelligence, is to slowly and methodically guide us through any predetermined lessons, which are seen as perfect ways to experience separation—betrayal, rejection, abandonment, abuse, rape, war, genocide, racial discrimination, and so on. It is also the job of the ego to see to it that the last piece of drama we create brings us to what can be seen as a breakdown phase. This breakdown experience is the signal for our Spiritual Intelligence to begin prompting us from deep within to ask such questions as the following:

> "Could there be something else going on that I can't see or have direct understanding of?"

> "Might there be a reason why this keeps happening to me over and over again?"

> "Could there possibly be some deeper meaning behind what is happening?"

At the same time, Spiritual Intelligence will guide us to a particular person, book, practice, or experience that might begin our awakening. Whatever it is that causes this initial movement, the purpose is to genuinely experience this breakdown period, which may last for many years, in order to get to a point where we begin to awaken to the truth of who we really are and why we are here.

It is my contention that you would not be reading this book if you were not already at the beginning point of awakening or in the midst of the process. Prior to this phase, your ego would have kept books like this out of your reach. Or if you had bought it, it would have remained unread until such time as your Higher Self said, "OK, time to read that book and begin waking up."

What I have noticed is that once people reach the awakening stage, their worldviews tend to change. Instead of a fixed materialistic/scientific point of view, they adopt one that is more metaphysical and open-ended. Their priorities begin to shift, as well—they tend to become more socially and environmentally aware, and they begin to see their purpose in life as being of service to others and to the world. They adopt an attitude of trust, a willingness to surrender to what life brings, and they emotionally relate to life with love rather than fear.

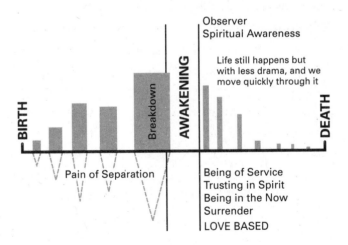

FIGURE 4 Timeline of Life Before and After Awakening

In figure 4 we see that after an awakening life goes on and things continue to happen as normal. But the difference is that, after the awakening, we don't create as many dramas, and for those that do occur, we move through them more quickly and have only a short emotional reaction to them. Peace comes much more readily than before, and life gets easier.

Once we reach the awakening stage, the dramas we created in the first half of life, in order to feel the pain of separation, are complete. This includes all of the instances when we acted as a perpetrator, as well as those when we were the victim. Such completion comes through the process of Radical Self-Forgiveness and Radical Self-Acceptance, which we'll continue examining in the following chapters.

8 Making an Apology

Whenever we have done something wrong and have caused harm or stress to another person or group of people, our natural impulse is to apologize. Should the apology be accepted, there is no doubt that this is helpful to us in the self-forgiveness process because it might take some of the heat out of the situation. We may even discover that the other party is not as aggrieved as we had expected, especially if we were indulging in a bout of inappropriate guilt. The other party may even be at pains to point this out to us and to persuade us that it wasn't our fault. That would give us an opportunity to jump-start the self-forgiveness process.

However, if the guilt is indeed appropriate and if the damage or injury done to the other party was severe enough, our apology might need to be extended to include some kind of atonement or amends process that represents a sincere attempt to make up for the hurt and pain inflicted. It may even call for some kind of restitution of previous conditions or reimbursement for what was lost. Financial reparations might even be called for as a form of compensation.

Whatever it is that requires such responses, we expect an apology to be calibrated to somehow *fit the crime*. In other words, it should be seen and felt to be appropriate and, hopefully, sufficient to begin relieving the injured party's pain and anguish over what happened. The principle of fairness comes into play here, together with a sense of justice, compassion, and human caring.

However, once again, we need to understand that just as there are two types of forgiveness—traditional forgiveness and Radical Forgiveness—there are also two forms of apology. As you would expect, there is an ordinary apology and a Radical Apology.

THE ORDINARY APOLOGY

An ordinary apology recognizes that a person was in some way damaged because of intentional wrongdoing on our part. It is a direct communication to the aggrieved party that we feel sorrow, guilt, and regret about the action or event and that we want to somehow make amends. This acknowledgment on our part may also be an appeal for forgiveness, although we must ensure that our apology doesn't become a form of manipulation. Apologies can easily become conditional and based upon our being forgiven, which means that they become more about us rather than the injured party. In other words, we apologize because we want to feel better.

It's important to note that ordinary apologies carry no undertone or recognition of an underlying spiritual purpose for what took place. If we were living in a fully awakened world where everyone was aware of the spiritual purpose behind all actions, there would be no need for an apology in the normal sense of the word, since nothing wrong ever happens. But we are not at that level of awakening yet—not by a long way—so apologies are still appropriate.

However, as individuals begin to awaken to the nature of the soul's journey and the divine purpose within everything, we also experience a subtle shift in how we make an apology. It's not that we say or do anything much differently than before; it's how we approach it that's different. I call this a Radical Apology.

THE RADICAL APOLOGY
A Radical Apology recognizes that someone was hurt and that this is something to be truly sorrowful for—perhaps even *appropriately* guilty about. We

also accept full responsibility for what happened in human and worldly terms and are willing to be accountable for what we have done. At the same time, however, we are open to the possibility that some higher purpose was being served and that it had to happen that way for some particular reason. We are, in effect, seeing the situation simultaneously from the perspective of both the World of Spirit and the World of Humanity.

We do not, however, communicate this perspective as part of our apology. It would seriously dilute our efforts in the eyes of the receiver, even if he or she had a similar metaphysical understanding, and would sound like an attempt to mitigate our pain and our guilt. We must be cautious about appearing to use spirituality as a way to avoid accountability and responsibility—a spiritual bypass, as we say.

Internally holding and honoring this perspective, however, will raise your own vibration. Remember, guilt and shame are very low vibrations. A willingness to be open to seeing spiritual perfection is a high vibration. The injured party will feel this vibration at some level and connect with it energetically. Such a connection has the ability to release the low-vibration energy tied up in the situation itself, thus enabling healing to occur more rapidly than with an ordinary apology. This type of healing will also contribute to an overall rise in consciousness such that, in the future, there will be less need for similar things to occur.

The sorrow and regret that are implied in any genuine apology are just as real with the Radical Apology. We feel this sorrow not so much because the wrong happened, but because the person, a fellow human being, was hurt or damaged. Acknowledging this sorrow opens the energy for Radical Forgiveness—especially for the victim. Therefore, a Radical Apology is a bridge to Radical Forgiveness and reconciliation.

The Radical Apology practice is also a step toward clearing our shadow. By simply bringing forth some rather unsavory parts of ourselves in committing this crime against someone else, we find love and acceptance for aspects within our own shadow that may have otherwise remained buried. In making the Radical Apology, we actually forgive ourselves for all of these hidden sources of shame.

The same is true for corporations, religious organizations, governments, and even countries. They all have their own shadows, many of them currently in need of healing. The United States, for example, has the issue of slavery, the Native American holocaust, continuing racial discrimination and injustice, and a whole host of other things for which it carries a significant amount of guilt and shame. Much of this shadow material remains suppressed or is subject to a strong sense of denial.

The interesting thing about this is that a country's shadow material can be healed by individuals doing the self-forgiveness work on behalf of the country. It works holographically. When one person raises his or her vibration, it raises the vibration of the whole. Once you recognize that your country's shadow is your shadow, too, you can do Radical Self-Forgiveness Worksheets as if you were the country itself. You can also make a Radical Apology to groups that your country has injured. Doing these things will shift the energy and move the overall energy in the general direction of healing.

So, we don't have to wait for our governments to act. We can make it happen ourselves. You can create your own apology, but here's one that I wrote for healing America:

Even though I know that everything was, is, and always will be in divine order, I/America am nevertheless now willing to make a blanket statement of Radical Apology to everyone and everything that I/

America have caused to be hurt or damaged in any way. I do this in the knowledge and comfort that this will begin the process of clearing my/America's shadow and, hopefully, healing the pain of those I/America have hurt. In particular, on behalf of all Americans, I put forth sincere Radical Apologies to:

☐ African Americans

☐ Native Americans

☐ Hispanics

☐ Chinese Americans

☐ Japanese Americans

☐ Other races _____

☐ Women

☐ Americans wrongly incarcerated
   and/or executed

☐ American citizens subjected to witchhunts

☐ The people of Nagasaki and Hiroshima

☐ The people of Vietnam, Afghanistan, and Iraq

☐ The people of other countries we have hurt by
   meddling in their affairs

You can make your own list or add something to this list that you feel strongly about.

Just as with our country, it is true, of course, that we are not directly responsible for what our ancestors did, and that what they did cannot be undone. The fact is that we are all carrying our ancestors' pain. If our forebearers were the victimized party, we carry their hurt and anger. If we are the descendants of the perpetrators, we carry their guilt and shame. All of these feelings are passed on to subsequent generations. There is no question that these cycles will continue with each generation in perpetuity until we decide to forgive ourselves and each other. It's completely up to us. The Radical Apology is the first step in that healing process.

9 The Radical Self-Forgiveness Worksheet

THE RADICAL SELF-FORGIVENESS WORKSHEET IS designed to help you work through and transform any guilt or self-recrimination about something that you might have done, or not done but should have. What follows in this chapter is the worksheet itself, along with some detailed explanations of each of the steps to help you understand what kind of response is being sought. This will help you get the most out of the process. You can also download a blank, letter-size version of the following worksheet from soundstrue.com/radicalforgiveness.

On a related note, it may seem silly, but the process becomes much more powerful if you read everything aloud—that is, everything provided in the worksheet, plus your written responses. A lot of energy is stuck in the throat chakra, so orating helps to move the energy.

HOW TO FILL OUT THE RADICAL SELF-FORGIVENESS WORKSHEET

Telling the Story
1.   What I am blaming myself for is . . .

_____

_____

_____

Telling the story is always the first step in any Radical Forgiveness process—in this case, it is the story of what you want to forgive yourself for. It's important to make a complete admission of what you have done. Make no excuses for yourself at this point, and do *not* overlay your story with any spiritual or psychological interpretation or reasoning. (That will come later.) Be as brutally honest as you can be. Don't hold back. Write as much as you wish; there is no space limitation on this section.

2.   **What I hear my judging self saying to me about it is . . .**

_____

_____

_____

Imagine yourself now as your critical, judging self. Really be the critic within and write all the things you need to say. Confront yourself. Be as nasty and vengeful as you want to be. Again, don't hold back and don't limit yourself as far as judgments are concerned. Allow yourself the full range of feelings and expression here.

Feeling the Feelings

3. **With regard to this situation . . .** (Circle as many as you judge appropriate to how you are feeling.)

a) **Toward myself, I feel:** *rejecting, dismissive, angry, distant, sarcastic, frustrated, critical, irritated, skeptical, ashamed, weak, sad, hurtful, hostile, angry, hateful, jealous, vengeful, rageful, apathetic, isolated, inferior, stupid, remorseful, lonely, depressed, ashamed, guilty, suicidal,* _____ , _____ , _____ , _____ .

b) **As I look at my life, I feel:** *apathetic, isolated, inferior, stupid, remorseful, tired, bored, lonely, depressed, ashamed, guilty, suicidal,*_____ , _____ , _____ , _____ .

c) **In general, I feel:** *bewildered, discouraged, insignificant, inadequate, hopeless, embarrassed, overwhelmed, confused, helpless, submissive, insecure, anxious,* _____ ,

_____ , _____ .

It is vitally important that you allow yourself to feel your feelings. Do not censor or repress them. Remember, we came into the physical realm to experience emotion—the essence of being human. All emotions are good, except when we deny them. Suppressing emotion creates potentially harmful energy blocks in our bodies. These blocks can cause all sorts of physical ailments, such as headaches, overall sensations of pain and discomfort, ulcers, and even cancer.

Self-Esteem Check

On a scale of 1–10 (1 being very low and 10 being very high), my self-esteem at this time is: _____.

It will be interesting to see how much your self-esteem might have risen by the time you have finished doing the worksheet, or even a day or two after. But first you need to have a feeling for what it might be at this particular moment so you have a benchmark. Just feel into it and enter a number that seems right to you.

4. **I lovingly recognize and accept my feelings, and judge them no more.**

☐ Willing   ☐ Open   ☐ Skeptical   ☐ Unwilling

Note: Check whichever box indicates most accurately your degree of willingness to accept this statement. There is no right one and, in fact, from an energy standpoint it makes no difference which one you check. It is just so you can assess where your consciousness is at this moment with regard to that statement.

This important step provides you with an opportunity to allow yourself some freedom from the belief that feelings like anger, shame, guilt, fear, jealousy, envy, or even sadness are bad and should be denied. No matter what they are, you need to feel your emotions in exactly the way they occur for you, for they are an expression of your true self. Your soul wants you to experience them fully. Know they are perfect and quit judging yourself for having them.

5. **I own my feelings. Since emotions are thoughts (or beliefs) attached to a feeling, my feelings**

are a reflection of how I see (judge) myself in relation to the situation.

☐ Willing ☐ Open ☐ Skeptical ☐ Unwilling

This statement reminds us that our emotions are our own, and that they provide us with important feedback about our beliefs. When we allow ourselves to feel, recognize, accept, and love our feelings unconditionally and know that they come from the parts of ourselves that need to be heard, we become merciful and loving toward those parts, even if we don't understand where they come from or what part of us is speaking at any particular moment. (It could be the inner critic, the wimp, the professor, the parent, or any one of a great number of the subpersonalities that live within us.)

Guilt Level Check

6. On a scale of 1–10 (1 being very low and 10 being very high), my guilt level at this time is: _____.

Notwithstanding the idea that everything is in divine order, we must realize and accept that, as a consequence of our choice to be human, we will be given the opportunity to experience, along with all the other emotions, guilt. It's all part of the divine plan.

Equally, it is part of the plan that we learn to be aware of and connected to our feelings and able to discern the subtle differences in their meaning. With guilt, we need to be able to discern the difference, for example, between what we are *entitled* to feel guilty about and that which we are not. In other words, to know the difference between appropriate and inappropriate guilt. Being able to discern this will save us a lot of confusion and pain, for most guilt is of the inappropriate variety.

Collapsing the Story

7. **My guilt over what happened is**
    appropriate/inappropriate. (Circle one and explain.)

    _____

    _____

    _____

    _____

    _____

    _____

Explain how you see this distinction applying to your particular situation.

Appropriate Guilt

When we have breached ethical and moral boundaries, broken laws, and/or committed acts that, by common agreement, are wrong, we are entitled to feel guilt. It is appropriate. For example, if we got drunk, drove recklessly, and killed someone, we are entitled to feel guilty about it.

Inappropriate Guilt

Inappropriate guilt is felt when we blame ourselves for something that we did not consciously choose, had no control over, no responsibility for, and for which we cannot reasonably be held accountable.

8. **Even though I don't know why or how, I now see that my soul has created this situation in order that I learn and grow.**

☐ Willing   ☐ Open   ☐ Skeptical   ☐ Unwilling

This is probably the most important statement on the worksheet. It reinforces the notion that thoughts, feelings, and beliefs create our experiences and that we order our reality in such a way as to support our spiritual growth. When we open ourselves to this truth, the problem almost always disappears. That's because there are no problems—only misperceptions.

The importance of this step comes in its ability to help you overcome the victim/perpetrator mode in order to open to the possibility that everything that happened or is happening was or is purposeful. It acknowledges that the divine essence within, the knowing part of yourself, your soul—whatever you want to call it—has aligned the situation so you can learn, grow, and heal a misperception or a false belief.

This step also creates self-empowerment. Once we realize we have created a situation, we also realize that we have the power to change it. We can choose to see ourselves as the villain in the situation, or we can choose to see that we have given ourselves (and any others involved) an opportunity to learn and grow, and then determine the way we want our lives to be.

The statement also challenges us to accept the possibility that the situation may be purposeful and to let go of the need to know how or why. This is where most intellectually inclined people have the greatest difficulty. They want proof before they believe anything. Therefore, they make "knowing why" a condition for accepting the situation as a healing opportunity. This is a dead-end trap, since to ask how and why things happen as they do is to ask to know the mind of God. At this current level of our spiritual development, we cannot possibly know the mind of God. We must, therefore, give up our need to know why (which is a victim's question, anyway) and surrender to the idea that God does not make mistakes, and therefore, everything is in divine order.

9. I am willing to see that my mission or "soul contract" included having experiences like this— for whatever reason.

☐ Willing   ☐ Open   ☐ Skeptical   ☐ Unwilling

A soul contract is an agreement that we made with other souls, prior to coming into the human experience, to carry out certain preplanned missions—to balance karmic energies, to heal group pain, to raise consciousness around some issue, and so on. Who could possibly know what the mission really was? We just need to be open to the possibility that the situation we have guilt around might have involved a soul contract, and if there are others involved in the situation, they may well have been the other souls with whom the contract was struck.

10. I now realize that nothing I, nor anyone else, has done or is doing is right or wrong. I drop all judgment.

☐ Willing   ☐ Open   ☐ Skeptical   ☐ Unwilling

This step goes against everything that we have ever been taught about being able to distinguish between right and wrong, good and evil. After all, the whole world gets divided along those lines. Yes, we know that the World of Humanity is really just an illusion, but that doesn't alter the fact that human experiences demand that we make these particular distinctions in our daily lives, as in the discussion on appropriate and inappropriate guilt.

Despite these distinctions, we must accept the idea that there is no right or wrong, good or bad, when seeing things from the spiritual big picture—from the perspective of the World of Spirit. From there, we are able to get beyond the evidence of our senses and minds, and we begin to see divine purpose and meaning in everything.

Once we are able to see the divine influence, we can understand that there is no right or wrong. It just is. There are truly no victims or perpetrators. We are all healing angels dedicated to each other's spiritual growth.

We experience this step differently in the process of Radical Self-Forgiveness than we do when forgiving others. We find it more reasonable to imagine that our being victimized is perfect in the sense that it was all part of the divine plan, than to accept that in our hurting someone else, there was also perfection. In Radical Self-Forgiveness, then, we seem to have to bring more effort to bear in allowing these to be equally true. If there are no victims, there can be no perpetrators.

11. I release the need to blame myself and to be right, and I am willing to see the perfection in what is, just the way it is.

☐ Willing   ☐ Open   ☐ Skeptical   ☐ Unwilling

This step confronts us with the perfection in the situation and tests our willingness to see this perfection. While it will never be easy to see the perfection, or good, in something bad that we have done, we must be willing to see the perfection in the situation, willing to drop the judgment, and willing to drop the need to be right.

It may always be difficult to recognize that, for instance, in abuse situations, both the abuser and the abused somehow created their situation so that each could learn a lesson at the soul level. It's possible that their mission was to transform the situation on behalf of all abused people. We must, nevertheless, be willing to entertain this thought. Obviously, the closer we are to a situation, the more difficult it becomes to see its perfection, but seeing the perfection does not mean understanding it. We cannot know the reasons things happen as they do; we must simply have faith that they are happening perfectly and for the highest good of all.

12. **Even though I may not know what, why, or how, I now realize that I and the others involved have been receiving exactly what we each had subconsciously chosen and we're doing a healing dance with and for each other.**

☐ Willing   ☐ Open   ☐ Skeptical   ☐ Unwilling

This statement serves as yet another reminder of how we can instantly become aware of our subconscious beliefs if we take note of what shows up in our lives. What we have at any particular point in time truly is what we want. We have, at the soul level, chosen our situations and experiences, and our choices are not wrong. And this is true for all parties involved in the drama. Remember, there are no villains or victims—just players. Each person in the situation is getting exactly what he or she wants. Each is engaged in a healing dance.

13. **I honor myself for being willing to play a part in others' healing and bless them for being willing to play a part in mine.**

☐ Willing   ☐ Open   ☐ Skeptical   ☐ Unwilling

This statement acknowledges that we have made an agreement to participate in the healing process with and for each other, perhaps as a preincarnation soul contract.

14. **I release from my consciousness all feelings of:**
    (As circled in #3.)

_____

_____

_____

_____

_____

_____

This enables you to affirm that you release the feelings that you had noted in section 3. Releasing emotions and corresponding thoughts serves an important role in the Radical Self-Forgiveness process. As long as those thoughts remain operative, they continue lending energy to our old belief systems, which created the reality we are now trying to transform. Affirming that we release both the feelings and the thoughts attached to them begins the healing process.

The emotions around a particular situation may come back time and time again—that's to be expected. Just be willing to feel them and then release them, at least for a moment or two, so the light of awareness can shine through you and allow you to see the misperception. Then, once again, you can choose to see the situation differently.

15. I honor my own willingness to see my misperceptions and bless myself for creating this opportunity to practice Radical Self-Forgiveness.

☐ Willing ☐ Open ☐ Skeptical ☐ Unwilling

This is another opportunity to feel gratitude and appreciation toward yourself for being willing to heal and grow through this process.

Reframing the Story

16. I now realize that what I was experiencing *(my perpetrator/victim story)* was a precise reflection of my human perception of the situation. I now understand that I can change this reality by simply being willing to see the spiritual perfection in the situation. For example . . . (Attempt a Radical Self-Forgiveness reframe.)

_____

_____

_____

_____

_____

This is likely to be a simple, general statement acknowledging that everything is actually perfect. In some circumstances, you can specifically match this declaration to the situation you're experiencing at the time, but more often than not, this will remain general.

If you are unable to see a new interpretation specific to your situation, that's not a problem. The Radical Self-Forgiveness reframe may simply be expressed in a very general way, such as: "What happened was simply the unfolding of a divine plan, which was called forth by my own Higher Self and those of the others involved to benefit my/our spiritual growth; and we were doing a healing dance with each other, so in truth, nothing wrong ever happened."

What would *not* be helpful would be to write an interpretation based on assumptions rooted in the World of Humanity, like giving reasons why it happened or making excuses. You might be exchanging one false story for another or even shifting into pseudoforgiveness.

A new interpretation of your situation should allow you to feel its perfection from the spiritual standpoint and to open to the gift you've been offered. Your reframe should provide a way of looking at your situation that reveals the hand of God, or Universal Intelligence, working for you and showing you how much it loves you.

Note: It may require completing many worksheets on the same issue to feel the perfection. Be absolutely honest with yourself, and always work from your true feelings. There are no right answers, no goals, no grades, and no required results here. The value lies in the process, in doing the work. Let whatever comes be perfect, and resist the urge to edit and evaluate what you write. You cannot do it incorrectly.

17. I completely forgive myself (your name),
    _____ , and accept myself
    as a loving, generous, and creative being. I
    release all need to hold on to negative emotions
    and ideas of low self-worth. I withdraw my
    energy from the past and release all barriers
    against the love and abundance that I know I
    have in this moment. I create my thoughts, my
    feelings, and my life, and I am empowered to
    be myself again, to unconditionally love and
    support myself, just the way I am, in all my
    power and magnificence.

The importance of this affirmation cannot be over-emphasized. Say it out loud and let yourself feel it. Let the words resonate within you.

If you sense resistance to believing this to be true about you, be willing to work through the resistance, knowing that on the other side lie peace and joy. Be willing also to feel any pain, depression, chaos, and confusion that may occur while you are going through it.

18. I now surrender to the Higher Power I think of
    as _____ and trust in the knowledge
    that this situation will continue to unfold

perfectly and in accordance with divine
guidance and spiritual law. I acknowledge my
oneness and feel myself totally reconnected
with my source. I am restored to my true nature,
which is love. I close my eyes in order to feel
the love that flows in my life and to feel the joy
that comes when the love is felt and expressed.

This represents the final step in the Radical Self-
Forgiveness process. However, it is not your step
to take. Affirm that you are willing to experience
it and turn the remainder of the process over to a
higher power. Ask that the healing be completed by
divine grace and that you be restored to your true
nature and reconnected to your source, both of
which are love.

This final step offers you the opportunity to drop
the words, the thoughts, and the concepts, and to
actually feel the love. The bottom line is, only love
exists. If you can truly tap into that love, you are
home free. You need do nothing else. So take a
few minutes to meditate on this statement and be
open to feeling the love. You may have to try this
exercise many times before you feel it, but one day,
just when you least expect it, the love and joy will
envelop you.

Integrating the Shift

19. A note to anyone who I hurt or negatively
    affected in some way:
    (name of person) _____ ,
    having done this worksheet, I now realize that
    there was a divine order to what happened.
    However, from the perspective of being in this
    physical world of pain and suffering, I still wish to
    apologize, to make amends, and to ask for your
    forgiveness. My Radical Apology is as follows:

    _____
    _____
    _____
    _____

20. A note to myself:

    _____
    _____
    _____
    _____

You began the Radical Self-Forgiveness Worksheet by
blaming yourself for something or feeling ashamed of
some part of you. Your energy has probably shifted

since you began, even if the shift occurred only a moment or two ago.

How do you feel about the situation now? What would you like to say to yourself? Allow yourself to write without conscious thought, if possible, and do not judge your words. Let them surprise even you. (Resist the temptation to go back to self-blame again.)

Maybe, as you acknowledge, accept, and love yourself unconditionally just the way you are, you will be able to release the perception of yourself as less than perfect. Perhaps you can accept that how you show up in the world represents the only way you can be. This is how Spirit has willed you to be.

After you have written the note, read the following statement out loud:

"I completely forgive you, (your name) _____ , for I now realize that you did nothing wrong and that everything is in divine order. I acknowledge, accept, and love you unconditionally just the way you are. I recognize that I am a spiritual being having a human experience, and I love and support myself in every aspect of my humanness."

Remember, all forgiveness starts as a fallacy. You begin the process without forgiveness in your heart, and then you "fake-it-till-you-make-it." So honor yourself for doing it, be gentle with yourself, and let the forgiveness process take as long as you need. Be patient. Acknowledge yourself for the courage it takes simply to attempt this Radical Self-Forgiveness Worksheet, for you truly face your demons in this process. Doing this work takes enormous courage, willingness, and faith.

When you have written the note to yourself, read this out loud: "I recognize that I am a spiritual being having a human experience, and I love and support myself in every aspect of my humanness."

Self Esteem Check
On a scale of 1–10 (1 being very low and 10 being very high), my self-esteem is now: _____.

It will be interesting to see the difference between this assessment of your self-esteem now that you have completed the worksheet with how you judged it to be at the beginning of section 3.

This is the end of the worksheet.

10 The Radical Self-Acceptance Worksheet

MUCH OF OUR SELF-ACCEPTANCE WORK has been started in the previous chapters. However, this chapter and the associated worksheet are great tools to use whenever you feel your judging self pulling you down and causing you to feel bad about yourself. The tools are a way to expose parts of your shadow that you have denied, repressed, or projected onto other people. By learning to recognize these parts, you can begin to love and accept them. You can also download a blank, letter-size version of the following worksheet from soundstrue.com/radicalforgiveness.

Recognizing your shadow parts is actually very simple, because people are always mirroring them back to you. You might recall the principle, "If you spot it, you've got it." This means that the qualities you find most objectionable in someone else are actually parts of yourself that you've denied, repressed, and projected, and that are now crying out to be loved and accepted.

HOW TO COMPLETE THE RADICAL SELF-ACCEPTANCE WORKSHEET

The beginning of the worksheet calls attention to our tendency to split ourselves into two parts—one side (image) containing attributes we have learned are acceptable, the other (shadow) side containing those that are not. Take a moment to recognize those that resonate most with you.

IMAGE _____ *versus* _____ SHADOW

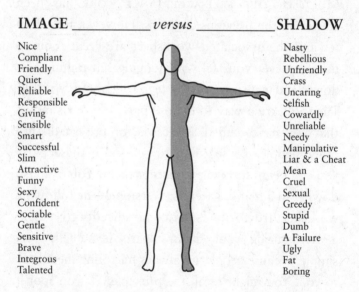

IMAGE	SHADOW
Nice	Nasty
Compliant	Rebellious
Friendly	Unfriendly
Quiet	Crass
Reliable	Uncaring
Responsible	Selfish
Giving	Cowardly
Sensible	Unreliable
Smart	Needy
Successful	Manipulative
Slim	Liar & a Cheat
Attractive	Mean
Funny	Cruel
Sexy	Sexual
Confident	Greedy
Sociable	Stupid
Gentle	Dumb
Sensitive	A Failure
Brave	Ugly
Integrous	Fat
Talented	Boring

1. **Write down as many "cool" attributes that you already accept as part of who you are. List all your good qualities, skills, talents, and gifts. Don't be shy. Really toot your horn!**

_____

_____

_____

2. What I am finding or have recently found
   objectionable in someone else that could easily
   be a part of my shadow, and that is crying out
   to be loved and accepted is:

_____

_____

_____

Write whatever it is that is upsetting you about
another person and see if you can possibly recognize that quality somewhere within yourself. Then
affirm that you love and accept that part of yourself.

3. (This is an alternative to section 2.)
   Even though no one is mirroring my shadow
   parts at the moment, I feel hatred toward
   myself. What I seem to hate most about myself
   right now is:

_____

_____

_____

Assuming you can identify it, write what seems to be showing up as the part of you that you loathe. If you're unable to identify it at this time, simply write that you don't know what it is.

Self-Esteem Check

4. On a scale of 1–10 (1 being very low and 10 being very high), my self-esteem is: _____.

5. Read the following statement out loud:
   I lovingly recognize and accept my feelings and judge them no more.

6. Read the following statement out loud:
   I own my feelings. No one can make me feel anything. My feelings are a reflection of how I see each situation.

7. Read the following statement out loud:
   I now realize that the shadow attributes that are being resonated within me, even when hard to recognize, are nothing more than stories I was shamed into believing were true. It is these that have caused me to feel poorly about myself. I now completely reject those stories and restore love to myself.

It's important to understand that even if someone is mirroring something to you, it is not always easy to see what the match is between their behavior and your shadow material. It is not necessary to know which shadow material is being activated, so don't feel obligated to spend a significant amount of time trying to discover what it is.

8. I now lovingly release all judgments and negative feelings about myself and totally accept myself just the way I am in all my (absolutely perfect) imperfection. In particular, I release the following:

_____

_____

_____

Write the same things here as you wrote in section 3. Remember, all forgiveness (and, thus, acceptance) is "fake-it-till-you-make-it," so don't worry if you don't feel self-love at this moment. The work is happening, even so. You must also note the perfection of your imperfection.

9. I realize that there are people I might be tempted to hold responsible for shaming me

into believing these stories and teaching me that I am less than perfect. I resolve to do as many Radical Forgiveness Worksheets as necessary to forgive them for doing this. (List the people.)

_____

_____

_____

_____

This could be an extremely important part of your process. As mentioned previously, it is usually our parents who, unintentionally for the most part, shame us into thinking ill of ourselves. Use the online Radical Forgiveness Worksheet at soundstrue.com/radicalforgiveness to clear this energy.

10. I would now realistically describe myself, with all my strengths and weaknesses, as follows:

_____

_____

_____

_____

Here, as you did on page 219, make a strong positive claim about who you are, including attributes that are considered unacceptable (shadow stuff) and those that are acceptable. Then state your acceptance of who you are, just the way you are.

11. **Read the following statement out loud:**
     I completely forgive myself, (your name)

     _____ , and accept myself
     as a loving, generous, creative being. I release all
     need to hold on to negative emotions and ideas of
     low self-worth. I withdraw my energy from the
     past and release all barriers against the love and
     abundance that I know I have already. I create
     my thoughts, my feelings, and my life and I am
     empowered to be myself again, to unconditionally
     love and support myself, just the way I am, in all
     my magnificence.

This proclamation, and the one that follows, are both very powerful statements of self-love and unconditional acceptance. Take a few moments at least to feel the love flowing through you once you have spoken the words. It would also be good to use them as the focus of a meditation whenever you are feeling low or self-critical.

12. Read the following statement out loud:

I now surrender to the Higher Power I think of as _____ , and trust in the knowledge that this situation will continue to unfold perfectly and in accordance with divine guidance and spiritual law. I acknowledge my oneness and feel myself totally reconnected with my source. I am restored to my true nature, which is love. I close my eyes in order to feel the love that flows in my life and to feel the joy that comes when the love is felt and expressed.

While the words are still resonating, see if you can in fact feel the joy, even if it is just a fleeting sensation. In the days ahead, as you continue to meditate on this and the preceding statement, that feeling will gradually increase.

13. A note to myself:

_____

_____

_____

_____

_____

Write some sort of loving statement to yourself saying how much you appreciate and honor yourself for doing the worksheet. Then finish by reading your statement out loud, as well as the following declaration:

I completely accept you just the way you are, for I now realize that you have always been perfect and that there was never anything wrong with you. I acknowledge, accept, and love you unconditionally just the way you are. I recognize that I am a spiritual being having a spiritual experience in a human body, and I love and support myself in every aspect of my humanness.

Self-Esteem Check
14. On a scale of 1–10 (1 being very low and 10 being very high), my self-esteem is: _____.

This is the end of the worksheet.

11 Radical Self-Forgiveness for Finances, Obesity, and Health Problems

PEOPLE BEAT THEMSELVES UP FOR lots of different reasons, but I think it is worth highlighting the two primary areas that seem to be the source of much self-inflicted guilt and shame for many people: finances and the body (especially obesity and health problems).

Regarding the body issue, we know from our work with Radical Forgiveness that what we find so objectionable about other people is simply a reflection of what we despise in ourselves. It is our own self-hatred projected outward. Equally common, and perhaps not so well understood, is our tendency to project our self-hatred onto our bodies. It is worth looking at how and why we do this, what effects this has on our health, and how we might take back the projection in order to find unconditional love for our physical self.

With the issue of finances, there is no doubt that people in general define their success in life (at least in the earlier phase of their lives, before becoming awakened) by how well they are able to accumulate money and create financial security for themselves and their families. With perhaps the exception of sexual prowess, men tend to gauge their entire self-worth by this measure. The question then arises, why is it that some people find it so easy to attract money while others do not, and does the Radical Self-Forgiveness technology offer a way to break through whatever blockage we might have around money? Let's look at this issue first and then come back to the body.

FINANCES

We have already seen that life in general, and people in particular, will always mirror back to us our beliefs, attitudes, prejudices, preferences, and whatever else resides in the subconscious mind. And yet, nothing reflects our subconscious programming more clearly than money.

If we accept the idea that we create our own reality with our thoughts and beliefs, then it follows that our financial situation is not a function of external forces, but of how we think and feel about money. This must also mean that if we change our consciousness around money, our finances will follow suit. Unfortunately, while that is true, it is more easily said than done. Our attitudes about money are extremely difficult to change.

We are strongly scripted from a very early age to see money in a certain way, and that programming is resistant to change. That's why most people go through life never varying a great deal with regard to income and wealth. We are very tightly programmed to stay within our money comfort zone, and as we discovered earlier, our saboteur self will do everything it can to make sure that we do. That's why, when people suddenly get a lot of money, they often lose it very quickly.

The answer to this problem lies not in trying to reprogram the subconscious mind (which is almost impossible anyway) or in making overtures to our saboteur self, but in using our Spiritual Intelligence to sidestep the subconscious mind altogether. We can accomplish this by using the Radical Self-Forgiveness process. Since that process includes a complete reframe, it enables us to slip easily into the new paradigm that says that money has no meaning other than that which we give it, that there is no shortage of money, that we can attract it whenever we want, and so on. This procedure should be enough to allow your Spiritual Intelligence to remove any blocks in the way of your solving whatever money situation you might have.

The benefits of Radical Self-Forgiveness with regard to money issues can best be achieved through the Three Letters Process. In the first letter, you tell your money story as it is occurring for you at the moment. In the second letter, you make some excuses for yourself and find all sorts of reasons why you are having the problems (old paradigm), which beliefs might be getting in the way, and so on. Then, in the third letter, you give expression to the idea that there is no shortage of money (new paradigm) and that you can attract the amount of money you need to dissolve what, until now, you thought was a real problem. Let me demonstrate how this might play out by way of a scenario that is all too common in today's times.

Let's assume that I am a middle-aged man accustomed to earning around $75,000 a year, but about a year ago I was promoted and had my salary increased to $95,000. About six months after that promotion, however, I lost my job and have been unable to replace it. Between my mortgage and other financial obligations, I practically lived paycheck to paycheck and, thus, had very little money in savings. I have been living on my credit cards since then and have run up a debt of about $60,000. Here's my first letter:

Letter #1

What a damn fool you have been. If only you had saved some money in case something like this happened. You just spent every bit of money every month without giving a thought to the future. Now look at you. You don't even have enough money to keep the car repaired so you can drive to interviews. You are headed toward bankruptcy, and you know it. The credit cards are maxed out, and all you can manage is to make the minimum payment. You know that will never be sufficient to get you out of debt in a hundred years. You are $60,000 in debt, and you can see no way out. Yes, you are feeling desperate, scared, and ashamed. Why wouldn't you?

The first letter explains the current situation without the slightest hint of sugarcoating. The situation seems pretty dire, doesn't it? The second letter might go something like this:

Letter #2

You know, you could fairly say that this has happened through no fault of your own. The firm got taken over, and despite the fact that the previous lot had just promoted you, the new people had different ideas about how the place should be run. So they let you go. And it's not surprising that you can't get a job, given the economic conditions right now. But you might have seen this coming. And you might have put some money away for a rainy day like this. But you were an optimist and always looked on the bright side, and had fun while you could. I always liked that about you.

But I guess you're now beginning to realize that there's more to this than meets the eye. Getting a big raise like that went to your head, didn't it? After all, you'd never had a raise of $20,000 before. It took you out of your comfort zone; that's what it did. And, as a result, you sabotaged yourself by losing your job. You were already pretty close to the top limit of your comfort zone at $75,000, so when you suddenly jumped to $95,000, things began to go awry.

You also didn't factor in that your parents taught you a lot of negative things with regard to money, which made you leery of having a lot of it. Your mother always said that people with money were crooked and likely to cheat you out of what you had, and you believed her. You didn't want to be thought of as untrustworthy. Your father was a working-class guy who earned a weekly wage, never thought he should or could get beyond his station in life, and hated people who did. He looked down on people who became "management," regarding them as traitors to their class.

He would have disapproved of your rise up the corporate ladder, especially since this last raise promoted you to junior management. You spent your whole life trying to win his approval, didn't you? The thought of his strong disapproval around this promotion was too much for you, so you found your way out.

Due to your father's seeming rejection, you have never felt worthy of much, have you? You probably felt that you didn't deserve that job either. Oh well—I guess you are at the mercy of events as they occur now and that the best you can hope for is a lucky break and a job offer. But you should look for something that pays no more than $75,000. Bankruptcy may be your only option.

The second letter represents a new understanding of why this has happened, the type of internal programming that is responsible for my fear of earning more than $75,000, and why my job subsequently disappeared once I was promoted. I am still strongly rooted in my victim role over it, but at least now I am able to take some responsibility for having a hand in creating the situation.

Now let's go to the third letter, which is the Radical Self-Forgiveness reframe letter.

Letter #3

Having come into this incarnation with the intention of creating opportunities to feel separation, you have done a wonderful job with this one. There's nothing like money issues to create separation.

Even though money has no inherent value or meaning, and there is absolutely no shortage of it, people tend to experience pain when separated from their money. And the more money one has, the more painful it is. Just the idea and fear of losing it is bad enough, let alone actually being separated from it. Therefore, money is a wonderful substance to help us feel our feelings and to learn and to grow in this area. People say they love money, but in actuality they hate it, because it generates so much fear of loss.

You have also become separated from your work, and all that you thought of as stable in your life has evaporated. You are, therefore, now in a wonderful position to discover humility, which is what you wanted to learn in this lifetime. If you go through bankruptcy, an undoubtedly humbling event, the experience will be tremendously valuable. You are also getting into that position where you have no choice but to surrender, so again, you have an opportunity to learn that lesson. There's so much to be gained in this whole experience.

At this point, you may also want to do a Radical Forgiveness Worksheet on your parents or anyone else who taught you negative things about money (visit soundstrue.com/radicalforgiveness). Completing this worksheet will help you realize how these people were serving you by establishing the groundwork that would set you up for this experience. You should feel a lot of gratitude for them having done this for you.

As your awakening process progresses, you will begin to understand that you can have as much money as you need, when you want it, and for whatever purpose. You will also learn that there are no victims or perpetrators and that the universe is a place of total abundance.

Let me assure you that the universe will shower its abundance upon you when you are ready to receive it. That said, you must first ask your Spiritual Intelligence to begin working with the Law of Attraction in order to generate this abundance.

I therefore suggest that when you finish this letter, say the following proclamations aloud:

1. "I now see myself as being in a heightened state of openness to receive money and to have resolved this situation in the most perfect way for all concerned."

2. "I now realize that I am someone who can, through the Law of Attraction, generate everything that I need in my life."

3. "I now turn this over to my own Spiritual Intelligence and surrender to Spirit in the knowledge and comfort that all is well and that what I saw as a problem was purely a misperception on my part. I have already resolved it by recognizing that I am abundantly supplied at all times. I now recognize that any idea of shortage or lack that I was holding on to has no validity or power whatsoever, and I give it none."

4. "I now realize that money was not the issue. I have no issues around money. Whatever the real issue was, I have handed it over to Spirit

and have an unshakable trust that Spirit will
take care of it for me."

It is my experience that when you use this technology
to break open a situation of this nature, magic happens. A job offer may simply come out of nowhere,
or a business opportunity could suddenly arise and
change everything. Maybe bankruptcy does occur,
but out of that experience comes a completely new
and financially rewarding life. You just never know.
The process is more potent than anyone can imagine, and even though I've been using it for years, I'm
still amazed by the results.

OBESITY

Body weight is the cause of much self-loathing, shame,
and guilt for a lot of people. Having said that, I am
addressing this section mainly to people who are sig-
nificantly overweight rather than people who feel
they just need to lose a few pounds. Nevertheless,
it is worth noting that, overweight or not, it is
extremely difficult to find anyone who is happy
with his or her body.

I pointed out earlier that it is possible that we have
come into this specific life scenario in order to experience separation, and all that goes with it, in order

to develop a deeper awareness of oneness. Also, in order to play the game, so to speak, we agreed to have spiritual amnesia. In other words, we would have no remembrance of the spiritual world from which we came. So, to us humans, the separation seems very real and, for the most part, very unpleasant. Not surprisingly, we try to avoid it. We agreed to experience separation, not just as a physical and mental phenomenon, but as an emotional event. And for that, a body was essential. Why?

Because an emotion is a thought attached to a feeling. Without a body to register the feelings, there would be only the thought. That would foil our intention to experience separation emotionally in order to eventually recognize the reality of oneness. That means the extent to which we won't allow ourselves to experience life through our feelings is the extent to which we are denying our purpose for being here.

Here's where it gets interesting. If the body is the vehicle responsible for taking us into and through the deep pain of separation, is it any wonder that we hate it for precisely that reason? Isn't it possible that a part of us might remember what it is like not to be encumbered with a body? Isn't it possible that we might have some resentment about having to carry this burden? If so, doesn't it make sense that we might project all our guilt and rage about being separate and in pain onto our body? After all, having taken on a body as a symbol of separation, it follows that the body must also symbolize the intense pain that inevitably accompanies the sense of separation.

In order to feel the pain of separation even more intensely within ourselves, we attract circumstances that will damage our bodies and wound us emotionally. Sexual abuse is one such example, and excess weight is often a clue that it has occurred. Even if the mind has blocked it out, the body remembers and accumulates fat as a layer of protection against a real or imagined future sexual attack. What better way to ward off physical advances than to make ourselves decidedly unattractive? What better way to become sexually unattractive than to be obese?

In this world of separation that we have created and live in, one of the ways to remain stuck is to consistently blame, justify, deny, and project the pain of having to endure separation onto something else. We do this in one of two ways: we either project it onto someone or something else, or we turn it back and project it onto our own body. Because we identify so closely with our body, the hatred we feel toward it becomes generalized as self-hatred.

However, once we have reached the stage of awakening and therefore no longer need to keep leveraging that pain, we can let go of the fear, knowing that we are safe and will not attract that experience anymore. At that point, the weight should come off, as it has for many people who have reported significant weight loss after completing this process.

From a Radical Self-Forgiveness point of view, there may still be several things for which you need to forgive yourself. For example:

1. Forgive yourself for attracting that circumstance into your life in the first place. By doing this, you are in effect taking responsibility for having a role in creating the situation, knowing that there are no accidents and that your soul creates such circumstances for good reason. If you are prone to guilt, you may have a tendency to turn against yourself and make yourself wrong; doing a Radical Self-Forgiveness Worksheet on this would be a way to guard against it.

2. Thinking that it was your fault. When children are abused, sexually or otherwise,

they often think they must have caused it in some way. This is compounded when, having summoned up the courage to tell their parents, they are disregarded or even chastised. Completing a Radical Self-Forgiveness Worksheet would help to dispel these thoughts. In this particular case, a Radical Forgiveness Worksheet on the parent would also be helpful.

3. Feeling guilty for any pleasure derived from the experience. Even though deep down a child knows it is wrong, stimulation of the genitals can still feel good. Nevertheless, this form of pleasure typically results in strong feelings of conflict and guilt. Since the body is made to feel pleasure, it is inappropriate guilt, which will be quickly recognized and addressed by completing a Radical Self-Forgiveness Worksheet.

4. For projecting your fear onto your body and, thus, gaining weight. The focus here would first be on forgiving yourself for misunderstanding that the fat was serving a very important function, and second, for

not realizing that adding fat to the most
vulnerable parts of your body was, in fact, a
self-loving thing to do.

Besides protecting against intimacy or sexual attack,
there are many other reasons for being overweight.
Even if we don't know the specific cause as of yet,
all we need to know now is that the body is crying
out for unconditional love. What is required in this
circumstance is to use the Radical Self-Acceptance
Worksheet, which helps us love and accept our body,
especially those parts of ourselves we have, up to
now, hated the most.

HEALTH PROBLEMS

Whenever we hurt ourselves or develop pain, disease, or malfunction in some part of our body, we
tend to project anger into that area. We do this for
more or less the same reasons I gave earlier in this
chapter—when our body lets us down, we feel victimized by it.

Once again, we are faced with that same question
I presented at the beginning of this book: who is
being victimized by whom here? (Is the body really
separate from who we are?) Even if we say that we
are not *just* our body, can we honestly say that it is

not an integral part of our human self? Might it not be more helpful to think of the body as just another aspect of self, just like the judging self, the ideal self, the inferred self, and all the others? Could it be that our victimization experience is simply the result of our body self being attacked by the judging self and the ideal self, both of whom say that we shouldn't be unhealthy and that ill health means we are failures?

What if we were able to see ill health as a self-created opportunity to feel separation within ourselves, just as we have qualified other forms of inner conflict? Isn't that how we quiet the judging self? Wouldn't that also mean that we might be more likely to release the ailment once we reach our goal for the amount of separation agreed to in this lifetime? Wouldn't we be more likely to release ill health by applying love and Radical Self-Forgiveness to our own body self if we saw it this way? Once we have awakened, wouldn't we have less need to even create ill health and disease?

Gregg Braden, in his book *The God Code,* presents a strong scientific case for God (as variously defined) being contained in our DNA. If this is true, then even when diseased our body cannot be other than perfect. In other words, as with everything about us, there is always perfection in our imperfection. And, in whatever form that imperfection shows itself, it is given to us, or chosen by us, as a way to grow and learn.

In his book *Your Soul's Plan,* Robert Schwartz shows quite conclusively that people choose to have certain physical and mental afflictions during their lifetimes in order to learn certain lessons. He verified this hypothesis by giving an outline of all his interviewees' stories to a psychic, a medium, and a channel. These three types of seers each independently gave very similar accounts for each person studied. Being able to see beyond the veil to the spiritual world, all three were able, in their own way, to describe a preincarnation conversation with each of the subjects' respective soul groups. The discussion centered on what each interviewee would choose to have for his or her life. The others would assist him or her by causing whatever circumstances he or she had chosen to come to fruition in some way.

The idea that the body has a consciousness of its own, which might be considered a self-within-the-self, is strongly suggested by Michael Talbot in his book *The Holographic Universe.* He recounts how he was having trouble with his spleen and began doing visualizations and other exercises in order to heal it. It wasn't working, so during a meditation he mentally scolded his spleen for not cooperating.

A few days later he visited a natural healer who was also a psychic. She was scanning his body, and stopped over his spleen and said, "Your spleen is very upset about something—have you been yelling at your spleen?" When he admitted he had, she became very cross with him.

"You mustn't do that," she said. "Your spleen thought it was doing the right thing by being ill, but when you scolded it, it got very confused. You should never be angry at your internal organs. Send them only loving messages."

These collective studies do seem to indicate that the body has a self that is intelligent and, yet, is still part of who we are. That gives us three possible ways of supporting it by applying forgiveness:

1. Treat the afflicted body part as if it were independently intelligent, and have a conversation with it. One way to do this, which is very effective, is to employ a practice known as Voice Dialogue. This technique was developed by the psychotherapists Hal and Sidra Stone as a way to dialogue with one's own subpersonalities.

To begin, sit in a chair with an empty chair opposite or beside you. Mentally place whatever part of yourself you want to dialogue with in the empty chair. Let's take the example of the spleen. With your eyes closed, ask your spleen what is going on. Then, immediately move to the other chair and provide an answer as if you were the spleen. Keep going back and forth, always shifting to the other chair each time you speak as either your authentic human self or your spleen. Keep your eyes closed for the entire exercise.

This practice has the effect of externalizing the part of the body that is afflicted, by making genuine dialogue possible in a way that would be precluded if you tried just to do it inside your head. You will be very surprised about what you learn from your body part by trying this technique.

2. Try a Radical Forgiveness Worksheet (soundstrue.com/radicalforgiveness). Having externalized the body part by employing the preceding methods, you can now use a Radical Forgiveness Worksheet

to forgive it for causing you pain. Through the practice of Voice Dialogue, you now have a forgiver (your authentic human self) and a forgiven (your body part).

3. Do a Radical Self-Forgiveness process in which you apply forgiveness to yourself for creating the health problem in the first place. This can be a Radical Self-Forgiveness Worksheet or the Three Letters Process.

Conclusion It's All
about Self-Love

I LAID OUT IN EARLIER chapters the theory that we
came here to experience the opposite of oneness
and love, in order to know oneness and love, and
that we would reach a certain point in our lives
when we would awaken and become aware of that
being our true purpose. Perhaps it has dawned
on you by now that your self-hatred was all part
of that plan. If that isn't yet clear to you, I invite
you to contemplate the idea. After all, what better
way to experience separation than to create wars
between aspects of your own self? Were not your
critical parent and resident judge serving you well
in keeping you from true self-love until you were
ready to become awakened?

Now that you have awakened (and I am certain
that you have—otherwise you would have thrown
this book away a long time ago), you can recognize that the divine purpose of the inner conflict has

been served and can now be dropped. From this point on, it's all about learning to love yourself just the way you are. You are a perfect expression of the Divine. You have always been, but you didn't know it until now. You are now about to come into the fullness of your divine nature as you journey on in your human body, loving yourself in your beautiful, divinely organized imperfection.

That's not to say that we won't encounter terrible acts and criminals along the way who will test our beliefs about this perfection—there will be times when we, too, are the criminal. However, these situations will give us the opportunity to reaffirm once more that, even though it doesn't always seem that way, in spiritual terms everyone is doing what they are supposed to be doing—sometimes for reasons known only to Spirit.

So if you are now, or have been, a criminal of some kind and are saying to yourself, "This cannot apply to me," know that it applies to you just as much as it does to the Dalai Lama or any other human being living on this planet. That means you are no less worthy of love than anyone else, and you can learn to love yourself no matter what. This self-love would almost certainly be an impossible task for any of us, especially as the criminal, were it not for the fact that we now have tools to use on a daily basis that will bring us ever closer to full acceptance of who we are, just the way we are.

We reviewed three examples in chapter 11 that show how the Radical Self-Forgiveness and Radical Self-Acceptance technologies can be applied for scenarios about which we tend to be most self-critical or apply an inordinate amount of self-blame. As you might suspect, I could have written chapter after chapter in the same vein, covering all sorts of examples, such as:

- Not having a life partner
- Being unable to have children
- Marrying the wrong person
- Missing the opportunity to . . .
- Not having the courage to . . .
- Criminal behavior
- Letting my friends down

But those examples would have been a waste of paper, because the prescription would be the same in every case: use the tools! It really is that simple.

Radical Self-Forgiveness frees us from traditional forgiveness in that it is quick, easy to do, and a simple step-by-step process. Your willingness to complete the worksheets with a relatively open mind is all that it takes. Your Spiritual Intelligence will take care of the rest. All of the principles and everything needed to activate your Spiritual Intelligence are embedded in the worksheets. That's why those are the primary tools in your toolbox.

The Three Letters Process is a little more challenging for some, since you must articulate some of these concepts in your own language and style; however, you'll soon find this freedom of expression to be exhilarating. Again, I want to assure you that your willingness to do the three letters is 99 percent of what is required. What you actually write is one small part of the process—even if your writing skills are not great, the universe will understand your intention.

I hope you have found these practical exercises enlightening, and that in discovering that you are an amalgam of many selves, you have come to know those parts of yourself better. I hope, too, that you can now love them just the way they are, no matter what. Finally, my wish for you is that you realize deep down that your I Am Self loves and supports you exactly as you are and recognizes you as the unique and wonderful human being that you are. I do, too.

I would like to finish the book with some words that are not my own, but I feel are fitting for the ending. I do not know who authored them, but I give thanks to the person who did.

The You That Is Special

In all the world there is nobody like you. Since the beginning of time, there has never been another person like you. Nobody has your smile. Nobody has your eyes, your nose, your hair, your hands, your voice. You are special.

No one sees things just as you do. In all of time there has been no one who laughs like you, no one who cries like you. And what makes you laugh and cry will never provoke identical laughter and tears from anybody else, ever.

You are the only one in all creation with your set of natural abilities. There will always be somebody who is better at one of the things you are good at, but no one in the universe can reach the quality of your combination of talents, ideas, natural abilities, and spiritual abilities.

Through all of eternity, no one will ever look, talk, walk, think, or do exactly as

you do. You are special. You are. And, as
in all rarity, there is great value. Because of
your great rare value, you need not attempt
to imitate others. You should accept—
celebrate—your differences and even those
parts of yourself that you judge to be not OK.

You are special. Continue to realize it's
not an accident that you are who you are.
Continue to see that you were created to
serve a very special purpose. Out of all the
billions of applicants for that mission, only
you qualified. You were the one with the
best combination of what it takes. Just as
surely as every snowflake that falls has a
perfect design and no two designs are the
same, so, too, are no two people the same.

Ask that you continue to be guided in
fulfilling your divine plan. Trust the process
and let it unfold in perfect sequence and in
perfect order. Be grateful and happy.

—Source unknown

References

Braden, Gregg. *The God Code.* Carlsbad, CA: Hay House, 2004.

Enright, Robert. *Forgiveness is a Choice.* Madison, WI: American Psychological Assn., 2001.

Griswold, Charles. *Forgiveness: A Philosophical Exploration.* New York: Cambridge University Press, 2007.

Hawkins, David R. PhD, MD. *Power vs. Force: The Hidden Determinants of Human Behavior.* Carlsbad, CA: Hay House, 1995.

Kappas, John G. PhD. *Relationship Strategies, The E&P Attraction.* Tarzan, CA: Panorama Publishing Company, 1992.

Lamott, Ann. *Grace (Eventually): Thoughts on Faith.* New York: Riverhead Trade/Penguin, 2008.

LeShan, Lawrence. *Cancer as a Turning Point: A Handbook for People with Cancer, Their Families and Health Professionals*. Bath, UK: Gateway Books, 1981.

McLuhan, Marshall. *Understanding Media: The Extensions of Man*. New York: MIT Press, 1992.

Patent, Arnold M. *You Can Have It All: A Simple Guide to a Joyful and Abundant Life*. New York: Simon & Schuster, 1995.

Piaget, Jean. *The Moral Judgment of the Child*. New York: Simon & Schuster, 1997.

Schwartz, Robert. *Your Soul's Plan: Discovering the Real Meaning of the Life You Planned Before You Were Born*. Berkeley, CA: Frog Books, 2009.

Simonton, O. Carl, Stephanie Matthews-Simonton, and James L. Creighton. *Getting Well Again: A Step-by-Step, Self-Help Guide to Overcoming Cancer for Patients and Their Families*. New York: Bantam, 1992.

Stone, Hal, PhD, and Sidra Stone, PhD. *Voice Dialogue*. Voice Dialogue International. 2009. Web. 7 June, 2010. delos-inc.com/index.htm

Talbot, Michael. *The Holographic Universe.* New York: Harper Collins, 1992.

Wong, Paul T. P. *Handbook of Multicultural Perspectives on Stress and Coping.* New York: Springer Publishing, 2005.

Reader's Discussion Questions

1. It is often said that in order to forgive others, you must first forgive yourself. To what extent to you agree with this idea? What are the arguments that run counter to this proposition?

2. "Our perfection lies in our imperfection." Explore the deeper meaning behind this seemingly paradoxical statement the author makes in this book. What does he mean by this assertion?

3. How do you think knowing your sexual self (as either an "emotional" or a "physical"), as well as that of your partner, might help improve or even save a relationship?

4. Discuss the many ways in which guilt can be inappropriate and see if you have some

instances in your own life where you have struggled to determine whether you were entitled to guilt or not.

5. Shame is induced by things our parents said or didn't say; did or didn't do. Whether they had intent to hurt you or not, you found them painful nevertheless, and it led to shame and low self-esteem. If you still carry that shame and see it impacting your life negatively, what are you prepared to do in order to heal the wounds and let go of the shame?

6. How would you go about sharing Radical Self-Forgiveness and Radical Self-Acceptance with another person who you knew was down on him/herself all the time, without adding to their shame?

7. Discuss the nature of "victim consciousness"— what it is; how do we support ourselves and others in being victims; what kind of mindset does it create and what price do we pay for holding onto blame, resentment, self-righteousness, and all the other aspects of victim consciousness?

8. When there is dissonance between our authentic self on the one hand and either, or both, our inferred self and ideal self, we experience anxiety about who we really are. Discuss how such incongruencies between our true self and these two external selves can arise and what can be done to alleviate the negative results.

9. What price do we pay for shutting down or trading away parts of our authentic self for things like wealth, status, recognition, power, love, acceptance by others, etc.? What parts of yourself have you traded away and what, if you had to do it over, would you never trade away again?

10. Take any situation that you might see on the TV or the news, and discuss whether the accused person is entitled to feel guilt—appropriate guilt—or is having to deal with projected or associated guilt that is in fact inappropriate.

11. Why do you think that virtually everyone, no matter how beautiful they might be, feels a strong measure of shame about their bodies and the way they look? How can this be changed?

12. Self-Acceptance is most difficult when it comes to loving our bodies exactly as they are. Why do we have such a hatred for this physical part of us and continually project onto it? Discuss ways in which we can come into loving resonance with our bodies, even when we are challenged with diseases like cancer.

About the Author

Born in England in 1941, Colin Tipping was raised during the war and in early post-war Britain by working-class parents. By his own account, his parents were good people, loving and hardworking, and he considers himself blessed in having had a stable and enjoyable childhood in spite of the social hardships of the time.

Even as a boy, he seemed to inspire the trust of people who needed to talk about their feelings, as they found in him a person who would listen and not judge. After a four-year stint in the Royal Air Force, he became a high school teacher and a college professor, but even then often found himself sought out to provide counseling for people.

He has three children from his first marriage, which ended in divorce after seven years. A second marriage lasted only four, but he nevertheless remains friends with both ex-wives.

He immigrated to America in 1984 and shortly thereafter became certified as a clinical hypnotherapist. He liked hypnotherapy because, after some years of experience, he concluded it sped up the therapy by a factor of at least three.

He was not religious then and still feels "free" of any organized religious dogma. His spirituality is essentially practical and down-to-earth, simple, free, and open-ended.

In 1992, he and his wife, JoAnn, who he met in Atlanta and married in 1990, created a series of healing retreats in the north Georgia mountains for people challenged by cancer. In recognizing that lack of forgiveness was a big part of the causation, they set about refining a new form of forgiveness that later was to become what is now recognized as Radical Forgiveness. Unlike traditional forgiveness, which takes many years and is universally seen as very difficult to achieve, this had to be be quick, easy to do, simple, and therapy-free.

In 1997, Colin wrote the first edition of *Radical Forgiveness*, and began doing workshops in January 1998. He now has an Institute for Radical Forgiveness in the United States, Australia, Poland, and Germany. He has no plans to retire.

For an interview between Colin Tipping and Tami Simon, Sounds True's publisher, please go to Soundstrue.com/bonus/Colin_Tipping_self.

96502